Do Alan, Kate, Mary, Siobhán, Caitríona agus Geraldine,
agus i ndílchuimhne Aonraí

Acknowledgements

It is said there's a season for everything, and now is the time for Ireland to tackle the growing issue of how best to care for its older people. Carer organisations, universities and government are working to adapt to this new global phenomenon. In this context, this book aims to provide a guide for those currently at the coalface of caring. I am very grateful to many people for making this book possible. Firstly, I would like to thank Orpen Press Commissioning Editor Dr Marie Murray. She was wonderfully encouraging and personally engaged throughout the publishing process, and I learnt much from her wise and compassionate input. I am deeply grateful to her and to Eileen O'Brien, Gerry Kelly and all the staff at Orpen Press. I also thank those who reviewed parts of the book and offered suggestions: Geraldine O'Dwyer, Patricia O'Connell and Kirsten Doherty. A big thank you also to Liam O'Sullivan and Zoe Hughes of Care Alliance Ireland, who offered help and support with the 'bigger picture' issues, and who are wonderful advocates for Ireland's family carers. Finally, a huge thank you to my family for their unconditional support throughout our own period of caring and through this writing process.

Foreword

Being a 'carer' for someone you love can be exceptionally rewarding, physically exhausting, emotionally heartrending, psychologically complex and socially isolating, depending on who you are caring for and the circumstances in which you become a carer. Caring can arouse ambivalent feelings: compassion, anxiety, resentment, guilt, grief, pity, anger, empathy, tenderness, irritability and envy of those who are free of this responsibility. It can be emotionally fulfilling or it can lead to burnout and compassion fatigue. It can be the most precious and profound life experience or the most daunting. It can unite families gloriously or tear them apart if the burden of care lies disproportionately or unjustly on certain members or if there is dispute about what is best for the person being cared for.

In this physical, psychological, emotional and time-management minefield of caring what is needed is a map through its terrain. *At the Coalface: A Family Guide to Caring for Older People in Ireland* by Máire O'Dwyer is just such a map. Designed to support the hundreds and thousands of people in this country who find themselves in a caring role, *At the Coalface* is a work of astonishing grace, practicality, professionalism and purpose, containing encyclopaedic information for readers about the realities of the caring role.

At a personal level I feel privileged to write the foreword to Máire O'Dwyer's book because of the altruistic spirit in which it is written by someone who is exceptional as a person, an author and an expert on the subject of caring through her personal experience and her work with Care Alliance

Ireland. It is also a privilege to be any part of a publication that will bring so much essential help to so many people at a crucial time in their lives.

When I first read the text of *At the Coalface* I was astounded by the breath, depth and wealth of information Máire had gathered over almost a decade of personal research on the subject. But the information in the book goes well beyond that of a formal researcher or writer, because it also derives from her own lived experience and that of her family as carers for her father during his declining years. It therefore addresses the subject of 'caring' in all its manifestations, from the moment caring begins until its natural end. The account of what is required at each stage is a gift that she and her family bestow on carers as Máire deals with every aspect of caring that people might need to know. And there is so much that people do need to know to cope with the multiplicity of demands that caring requires. I think this book contains them all!

One of the major problems with caring for an older person, as *At the Coalface* points out, 'is the huge uncertainty that affects many aspects of the caring situation – how much and when an older person's functioning will decline, how far their needs will extend, how long the caring situation will continue, how the family carers will cope' and whether the available finances will last. Additionally, those who find themselves in caring roles are not a homogeneous group – they may be people at different life-cycle stages with different financial means and personal resources, with a multiplicity of other work, home, children, family, personal and relational responsibilities.

Despite there being many organisations, websites and publications which provide excellent information on all aspects of caring, such as the Health Service Executive (HSE), Family Carers Ireland (FCI), the Citizens Information Service and Care Alliance Ireland, which is the umbrella organisation for all carer organisations in Ireland, as Máire points out, 'finding the *exact* information needed in a particular situation can be extremely time-consuming and exhausting'. This is where *At the Coalface* comes into its own because it literally does the work for you. A scroll through the table of contents shows how logically, comprehensively and accessibly the information in the book is laid out. The introduction sets the context in which caring arises and develops and how it is a critical issue at this historical juncture when most of us are likely to find ourselves both in caring roles and subsequently having to be cared for by others. Covid has also shone a light on the need to review how we care for people and the options offered to them. It has shown that what is available for many is not enough, that carers require more respect, respite and realistic remuneration for what they do, with greater legislative backing and implementation of the long-promised Statutory Home Care Scheme, which, as Máire notes, now needs to be made an urgent priority by government in 'a fair and easy-to-access national system of support for older people and their family carers'.

The book itself is divided into seven parts, each dealing with a separate aspect of caring for the older person. The introductory section shows how sequential and alarmingly incremental the process of caring can be. For example, Máire writes about the initial signs that help is needed: caring that starts after a hospital stay; gradual loss of independence and how it is measured; risk factors and cognitive decline. Part II brings the reader through every aspect of working with the public health system, such as universal and means-tested care; home support services; care needs assessment; day centres and community respite. There is an invaluable section on organising medical appointments in addition to information on safe driving, mobility parking permits, security in the home, burglar alarms and panic buttons.

A sensitive area is managing finances and legal issues, and the building of trust when assistance is needed, especially if power of attorney has to be organised. This is another minefield through which Máire guides the reader, step by step, with exquisite sensitivity. She describes safe financial management; witnesses for documentation; Local Property Tax exemptions; tax relief; grants and all the legal nuances right down to Advanced Healthcare Directives (AHD) that an older person may wish to have.

But there are further dimensions to this book which lie in the compassionate manner in which it deals with the emotional aspects of caring, with natural love and affection, with the pain of empathy watching someone you love decline, with the hurt of their irascibility, or the overwhelming feelings of tenderness a dependent person's gratitude can evoke. There is anticipatory grief, with inevitable guilt no matter how much one does, as carers are often torn in so many directions simultaneously. There is the carer's relationship with spouse or partner, with their children; the older person's relationship with grandchildren; sibling relationships within and friendships outside the family; and, most importantly, self-care for the carer. Indeed, this might be where readers who are carers should initially dip into this book, so that before they care for others they resource themselves.

The psychological sadness and stress of dealing with the incremental losses parents suffer, their reduced capacities and increased dependency, the poignant role reversal that occurs in child–parent dynamics, the profundity of the emotions about life and death, meaning and mortality that caring for others evokes are inescapably acute. But despite its trials and complexities, being a carer is also a demonstration of humanity at its best: unconditional love, personal duty, filial respect, familial loyalty and faithfulness that can allow carer and cared for to experience themselves and the meaning of life in profound ways. This is not to idealise it – but perhaps to reference the extraordinary, selfless, compassionate work done by so many people in our society and how much they deserve adequate support and services to assist them in what they do. This is something that all of us, backed by government investment, need to prepare for so that we can care for others and, in time, be cared for ourselves with appropriate social services, medical attention and proper respite intervention for our carers too.

At the Coalface: A Family Guide to Caring for Older People in Ireland by Máire O'Dwyer is the A to Z of caring – the carer's dictionary and directory, manual, handbook, map and guide to take the stress out of searching and replace it with compassionate care for carers who need not just to mind others but to be minded themselves. This is what this book does. It minds the minder, cherishes the carer and offers a helping hand to make an often overwhelming task manageable. Who cares? We do.

Dr Marie Murray
Clinical Psychologist, Systemic Psychotherapist and Author
Health Publications and Commissioning Editor, Orpen Press
@DrMarieMurray

Contents

List of figures

List of tables

List of checklists

Table of abbreviations

AAL	Ambient assisted living
ADL	Activities of daily living
AHD	Advance Healthcare Directive
CPR	Cardiopulmonary resuscitation
CSAR	Common Summary Assessment Report
CSO	Central Statistics Office
CSPE	Civil, Social and Political Education
DEASP	Department of Employment Affairs and Social Protection
DNR	Do Not Resuscitate
EFT	Electronic funds transfer
EPA	Enduring Power of Attorney
ESRI	Economic and Social Research Institute
FCI	Family Carers Ireland
FETAC	Further Education Training and Awards Council
GP	General practitioner
HIQA	Health Information and Quality Authority
HCP	Home Care Package
HSE	Health Services Executive
HSS	Home Support Service
INR	International Normalised Ratio
LPT	Local Property Tax
MMSE	Mini Mental State Examination

MSOP	Manager of Services for Older Persons
NCPOP	National Council for the Protection of Older People
NCT	National Car Test
NHS	National Health Service
NHSS	Nursing Homes Support Scheme
OT	Occupational Therapist
PHN	Public Health Nurse
PRSI	Pay Related Social Insurance
RPM	Remote Patient Monitoring
RTP	Rural Transport Programme
SOP	Services for Older People
TILDA	The Irish Longitudinal Study on Ageing
USC	Universal Social Charge
VAT	Value Added Tax

Glossary of terms

Term	Meaning
Advance healthcare directive	A directive about the type of healthcare treatment a person may want in the future should they be unable to make relevant decisions on their care at any time.
Care needs assessment	An assessment carried out by a health professional to establish the level of care that an older person needs.
Carer needs assessment	An assessment of the needs and health of family carers. No such assessment is currently made in Ireland, although other countries have such schemes in place.
Care worker/ home care worker	A professional who provides care at home for an older person. These can be employed by agencies or directly by older people and their families.
Community Intervention Team	HSE teams that provide certain medical services at home for older people, avoiding the need for them to attend clinics.

Day centre	Day centres are part of the public system of care for older people. They are centres that older people can attend during the day for classes, meals and other activities.
Do not resuscitate order	An indication in writing by a person that they do not want extraordinary measures taken in the event of a medical emergency. This is generally taken to mean cardiopulmonary resuscitation (CPR) in the case of cardiopulmonary failure.
Enduring power of attorney	An enduring power of attorney (EPA) is a special form of power of attorney that takes effect only when the person giving the power (the donor) becomes incapacitated.
Family carer (also previously known as 'informal carer')	A family member or friend who cares for an older person on a regular and unpaid basis (although those receiving Carer's Allowance or Benefit are included in this definition). The term 'informal carer' was previously used but the HSE and carers organisations have agreed to discontinue its use.
Health Information and Quality Authority	The independent authority established 'to drive high-quality and safe care for people using our health and social care services in Ireland'.
Home help	The name previously given to care provided by the HSE to older people with good levels of functioning. Home help often referred to household tasks as opposed to personal care.
Home Care Package	The name given to the package of care provided to an older person by the HSE. It can include home care hours, services such as physiotherapy and occupational therapy, respite, etc.

Home Support Service	The new name (2018) for the HSE's service providing care at home to older people. The Home Support Service covers the previous home help, Home Care Package and Intensive Home Care Package services.
Nursing Homes Support Scheme	A government scheme by which the costs of care in a nursing home are shared between the older person and the state.
Respite	Respite care is provided as part of the HSE's Home Support Service. It allows the older person to move to a local community hospital for a week or two so that their carers can have a break from their caring responsibilities.
Telecare	Telecare is technology used to aid in the provision of care. It can include monitors and sensors including motion or fall detectors, fire and gas alarms, location devices to find a person who has wandered off, etc.
Telehealth	Telehealth is the use of technology to provide health services and distribute information. It can include wearable monitoring devices, and video hubs allowing video calls to medical professionals.

Part I

An Introduction to Caring for an Older Person

1

Introduction and about this book

The ancient Irish had an enlightened attitude to looking after older people. Three types of care or 'maintenance'[1] were required: 'maintenance in food, maintenance in attendance, maintenance in milk'. In practical terms this translated to 'half a cake of wheaten meal, with salt; and a vessel of sour milk' daily and the obligation to 'wash his body every twentieth night, and to wash his head every Saturday'. A millennium and a half later, we still need similar care.

This book came to be for two reasons. The main one was my own family's experience of caring for our father over a period of almost ten years. Like most older people, he wanted to be cared for at home, and we also wanted to keep him at home. As he grew more frail and dependent we

---

[1]   O'Curry, E. (1873) *On the Manners and Customs of the Ancient Irish*, Volume 3.

found ourselves dealing with situations we could never have imagined, and becoming involved with the public health system with all its intricacies and bewildering complexity. We were lucky to have the support of a wonderful public health nurse and primary care team, but despite this, the learning curve was huge; we often felt lost in a fog of information, unsure where to turn. What we wouldn't have given for a guide through the mist, the medical issues, the professionals involved, the care options, the costs, and so on.

The second motivation for this book came from my work with Care Alliance Ireland. Care Alliance is the umbrella organisation for all carer organisations in Ireland. It advocates for family carers at government level; collaborates with universities on research relevant to carers; and provides practical help to carers through its publications, website and annual Carers Week. I have worked with Care Alliance on reports, surveys, discussion papers and submissions to government over a number of years. I have been privileged to see the excellent work carried out by highly motivated people – many of them carers themselves – in various carer organisations.

So, in essence, I know the theory and have also seen first-hand how policy translates into practical resources and services at the coalface.

Populations around the world are ageing as modern medicine and technology prolong life far beyond previous limits. But with increasing age comes, for many, increasing health problems and increasing care needs. Governments are having to reassess how they provide care for older people, and how they help families care for their relatives. The situation is unprecedented in human history. Although there have always been people who have lived into their 80s, 90s or even hundreds, these have been a minority. Now, at least in the Western world, general life expectancy extends into the 80s – in Ireland in 2015 it was 81.5 years, while in 1990, just 25 years previously, it was 74.7 years. That is an increase of almost seven years in just two-and-a-half decades. The challenge is a global one, and every country is grappling with the question of how best to look after older people. In Ireland, we are just beginning to examine in earnest the reality that many if not most of us will experience a long period of 'old age', and require help and care from family and the state during that time. It is a reality that is unlikely to change. People who read this book today as carers are likely to experience the other side of the coin – as care recipients – in the future. It is also true that many more people today than in the past will spend periods of their lives as family carers. So, this new phenomenon will touch all of us in the years ahead, and for that reason we as a society must plan and implement now the best possible system of care and support for older people and their family carers.

In May 2019 Family Carers Ireland (FCI) released a major report which found a '*severe disimprovement* in the wellbeing of family carers over the past decade, along with a huge increase in the burden of caring'.[2] FCI has called the period 2009–2019 'a decade lost' and says that in this period 'carers have poorer health, less support and are more worried about the future', while President of the College of Psychiatrists of Ireland Dr John Hillery called the results 'scandalous'. As we discuss in the book, plans for a new statutory home care scheme are ongoing in the Department of Health, and legislation is due to be delivered in 2021, although the Covid-19 pandemic has caused a delay. In the meantime, family carers are bearing the brunt as the state encourages more people to become economically active in the workplace, reducing the pool of family carers, while increased spending on care fails to keep pace with demographic changes.

ADDENDUM

The book was written before the Covid-19 pandemic began in late February 2020 and readers should note that some supports may not be available during the pandemic or may have moved online. The pandemic has upended much in our world, including the care of older people in Ireland. The horrifying impact of Covid-19 on nursing homes has focused attention on the care of older people like never before. Many families are now frightened to consider residential care for their older relatives and will turn instead to how they can manage home care. In this context the statutory home care scheme should be made an urgent priority by government. When work on the scheme started it was intended to put home care on a statutory footing and to increase regulation in the sector, but it was expected that the current home care/nursing home model would for the most part continue as is. However, in recent months there have been numerous calls for the nursing

---

2   Family Carers Ireland, the College of Psychiatrists of Ireland and the UCD School of Nursing, Midwifery & Health Systems, 'Paying the Price: The Physical, Mental and Psychological Impact of Caring': https://familycarers.ie/media/1421/paying-the-price-the-physical-mental-and-psychological-impact-of-caring.pdf.

home model to be replaced or substituted in the wake of Covid-19.[3] Former Taoiseach Leo Varadkar is among those who have raised the question of the future care of our older population (*Late Late Show*, 8 May 2020).

The debate is likely to continue, but as with so many issues, ordinary people will make their own decisions and leap ahead of the debate. Many families will choose home care for their older relatives if at all possible and I hope that the information in the book will make that an easier task. However, for the time being nursing homes form part of the care of older people in Ireland, and over the next few years there will continue to be very frail people who require intensive nursing care that may be impossible to provide in a home environment. Despite the havoc that the pandemic has brought, we can be sure that there are many nursing homes run by competent, kind and compassionate staff and owners. As we discuss later in the book, the best way to ensure good care in nursing homes is for relatives to be visible and involved in care, by visiting, asking questions and assisting staff in making the care the best it can be. We can only hope that the tragedies that affected so many families around the country will ultimately result in a review of what went wrong and new thinking on how to improve all care of older people.

THE AIMS OF THE BOOK

Saving time, saving stress

One of the major problems with caring for an older person is the huge uncertainty that affects many aspects of the caring situation – uncertainty about how much and when an older person's functioning will decline, how far their needs will extend, how long the caring situation will continue, how the family carers will cope, and how long available finances will last. While caring for a short period is difficult – it may result from a sudden illness or accident and be shocking and difficult to come to terms with – caring over a long period is debilitating. Every person has limited mental, physical and emotional resources, and these become depleted over time. Caring for a person with significant needs, particularly someone at 'end of life', is recognised as a continuing state of trauma. It may be on the lower end of the trauma scale,

---

[3]   https://www.irishtimes.com/opinion/nursing-homes-must-be-made-a-thing-of-the-past-1.4257422.

but it is trauma nonetheless. In addition, many carers have multiple responsibilities – they may be employed or run businesses; they many have young children or teenagers; they may be caring for another older person (perhaps the parent of a spouse/partner); they may be involved in civic, sports or other organisations. All of these also take a share of the carer's physical, mental and emotional resources. And of course, time is a big issue; there are only so many hours in a day. Caring is hugely labour intensive; no matter how organised you are, something will invariably arise to eat away at your carefully planned schedule. It may be something as simple and frustrating as a lost pair of glasses; it may be calming the older person if they become distressed; it may be discovering that the heating is playing up. Many carers who are highly organised and capable people discover that the care of an older person with high care needs is only partially within their control; for much of the time they are firefighting.

This leads to the primary motivation for this book – saving time and effort for carers. A recent paper[4] studied the effort required by carers in navigating the care system, i.e. finding, applying for and accessing supports and services. The authors called this effort the 'structural burden'. They found three main challenges:

- **Digging and hunting:** the effort involved in finding out what options are available and how to access them
- **Pushing through and working around:** this describes how, even when carers find available supports, they have to 'push through' and 'work around' obstacles. The authors say: 'where caregivers encountered inflexible, overly complex policies, restrictive eligibility, or long waits … [t]o get what they needed, caregivers had to actively and persistently advocate for their needs or find alternative solutions.'[5]

---

[4]   Funk, L.M., Dansereau L., Novek S. (2017) 'Carers as System Navigators: Exploring Source, Processes and Outcomes of Structural Burden', *The Gerontologist*, 59(3): 426-435. https://academic.oup.com/gerontologist/article-abstract/59/3/426/4641800?redirectedFrom=fulltext.

[5]   'Lost at Sea: Caregivers Stressed by Navigating Support Systems', *The Mather Institute for Ageing*, 4 December 2017, available from: https://www.matherinstitute.com/2017/12/04/caregiving-support-systems-are-stressing-out-caregivers/.

- **Navigating fragmentation:** the third aspect of the structural burden of caring is having to bring services and systems together: '[the need to] coordinate services and ensure a smooth flow of care. Here, caregivers must link various services systems ... This requires them to be organised and diligent in coordinating and monitoring care.'[6]

Digging and hunting

A multitude of organisations, websites and publications provide excellent information on all aspects of caring. In particular, the Health Service Executive (HSE), the carer support organisations including FCI and Care Alliance Ireland, and the Citizens Information Service provide invaluable information. However, finding the *exact* information needed in a particular situation is time-consuming and sometimes difficult. You may start at the home page of a website and find the information you need 20 minutes later. There are a multitude of publications available from organisations, but having diligently read many, you can still wind up with only a fragmented picture of any given situation. This book aims to provide an 'A to Z' of caring, gathering information from resources far and wide and presenting it in a manner that makes it easy to find the exact information you need at the precise time you need it, saving time and effort.

The book also explores in some detail the emotional aspects of caring – the relationships that are affected by a caring situation within a family; the conflicts that may arise; the worry, grief and guilt that family carers commonly feel. Also explored are ways to self-care – steps that people can take to look after themselves as they care for their older relative or friend.

In essence, the book attempts primarily to do two things: firstly, to gather and present the available information in an easy-to-read, logical format, and secondly, to deal with the problems that arise for carers in a practical, step-by-step manner. One particular challenge for carers is knowing *who* to turn to for a specific form of help. Knowing who provides which service and how to access it is essential in dealing quickly and effectively with changing care problems and avoiding constant firefighting. This book is intended to help carers with some of these challenges by providing guidance on options and by directing them straight to the relevant resources. This is done by

---

[6]   'Lost at sea', *The Mather Institute for Ageing*.

giving details of the person or organisation that can provide a particular support, with relevant web links and contact details. Where information on a particular issue is available on an organisation's website or in a publication, those precise sections are pinpointed throughout the book. In this way much of the 'digging and hunting' described above can be avoided.

Pushing through and working around
It is hoped that some of the very practical workarounds provided in this book will help where obstacles are encountered in dealing with public bodies or other organisations. An example is the requirement to provide a passport or driving licence as identification for many services or when dealing with financial institutions – these are documents many older people no longer have. You may need to convince the management of the service or organisation to accept substitute documents; this way the problem can be 'worked around'.

The management chain in certain areas relevant to home care is outlined, so if obstacles are found at one level, a carer can move to the next level up to try to progress the issue. For example, if problems are encountered in accessing a Home Care Package (HCP), carers can contact the Manager of Services for Older People (MSOP) within their local authority. The focus throughout this book is on practical solutions. This addresses the 'pushing through and working around' part of the structural burden.

Navigating fragmentation
The final part of the structural burden of finding and obtaining support is 'navigating fragmentation', or coordinating all sources of help and support. This may involve interaction with multiple health professionals, with hospitals, with private home care agencies, etc. Part II of the book deals with this aspect, with chapters on working with the public health system (Chapter 4), everyday caring (Chapter 5), dealing with medical issues and more complex needs (Chapter 6), and with problems particular to older people (Chapter 7).

One difficulty that can arise for carers navigating the system is that services and the staff who administer them currently vary by geographic area. These discrepancies have resulted both in an unequal distribution of scarce resources and in complications communicating services to the public. A process is currently underway at government level and in the HSE to remove these geographic differences (the 'postcode lottery') from the system by moving toward a nationwide system of care based on legislation. These efforts are welcomed by family carer organisations, but this development, which was due in 2021, has been impacted by the Covid-19 pandemic and may be further delayed.

In the meantime, family carers feel abandoned to their fate. For many, that fate feels like an extreme lack of time and a superabundance of stress. It may be a cliché, but the metaphor of being offered a sticking plaster to cover a gaping wound is apt. As any carer will tell you, there are 168 hours in a week (24 hours x 7 days). The current allocation of home care hours, especially for those at end of life who need round-the-clock care, does little to meet the needs of the situation.

It takes a village

Carers may need the patience of a saint, the diplomacy of the United Nations, the compassion of Gandhi, the 'zen' of the Dalai Lama and the resilience of Nelson Mandela. A huge dose of common sense is also essential. Unfortunately, few of us are equipped with all of these attributes. However, we are all part of communities – friends, neighbours and extended families; we shop in local businesses and bank in local banks; we have local public services such as the Gardaí and libraries. A second aim of this book is to encourage Irish society to 'share the care' in a much more expansive way. Businesses and public services need to examine how they can improve their services to carers and older people who are their customers and neighbours. Chapter 5 includes a list of suggested ways in which communities can participate in caring for their older members. There is no doubt that in the near future the answer to the question 'Who cares?' is likely to be 'All of us'. Most people are likely to experience a period of caring during their lifetime. It is said that it takes a village to raise a child; the same can be said of caring for an older person.

HOW THE BOOK IS ARRANGED

The book is divided into seven parts, each focusing on a separate aspect of caring for an older person:

Part I of the book is an introduction to the world of caring in three chapters. Chapter 2 deals with the beginning of caring – how to recognise when an older person is losing independence, and when you have effectively become a carer. Chapter 3 discusses the conflict between what an individual who is becoming unable to live independently wants and what they need. It also details the common ways in which dependence increases, and the tools used by health professionals to measure a person's level of dependence. It examines common and more extensive care needs.

Part II (Chapters 4 to 7) offers a foundation in the main aspects of caring, from dealing with the public health system to practical ways of handling common problems. Chapter 4 discusses the current health system in relation to the care of older people. It looks at the role of public health nurses and local primary care teams, and examines the current system of Home Care Packages. Practical guidance is given on how to work with the public health system to provide the best care for your relative. Chapters 5 to 7 deal with the practical side of caring. Chapter 5 looks at basic day-to-day care, suggesting solutions to common problems such as keeping an older person supplied with healthy meals and managing hygiene. Chapter 6 continues with more complex care needs, including ways of managing chronic health conditions at home with the help of the HSE community intervention team. Chapter 7 examines particular issues that can arise, such as cognitive impairment or difficulties with communication, and issues relating to mobility and security at home.

Part III (Chapters 8 and 9) discusses finances, managing an older person's home and legal issues. Chapter 8 examines managing the home and/or finances, while Chapter 9 examines legal issues such as the Enduring

Power of Attorney (EPA), Advance Healthcare Directives (AHD) and Do Not Resuscitate (DNR) orders.

Part IV (Chapters 10 and 11) moves on to getting extra help. Chapter 10 looks at the help available from carers organisations and at aspects of hiring care workers privately, including which questions to ask and how to check Garda vetting. Chapter 11 gives details of various grants available through local authorities, including the Home Adaptations Grant and the Mobility Aids Grant Scheme. It also explains the Fair Deal scheme and provides practical guidance on applying for this scheme.

Part V (Chapters 12 and 13) looks at relationships and the emotional aspects of caring. Chapter 12 examines the various emotions that carers experience, ranging from love to guilt, worry and grief. Chapter 13 discusses the effects on relationships within the wider family, and ways to manage the division of care between family members. This chapter also deals with the need to accept help, and discusses the difficult issue of an older person expressing a wish to die.

Part VI (Chapters 14 and 15) deals with coping and self-care. Chapter 14 examines various coping strategies, while Chapter 15 is devoted to self-care for the carer.

Part VII (Chapters 16 to 18) looks at what happens when caring ends, and the issues of compassion fatigue and carer burnout. Chapter 17 discusses alternatives to family care at home, including paid 24-hour care at home and residential care. It pays particular attention to how family carers can continue to care for their relative when they are living in a nursing home, albeit in a different way. Finally, Chapter 18 looks at the impact of an older person's death, and life after caring.

NOTE ON TERMS AND USAGE

In writing about caring I am very aware that I am writing about issues of enormous sensitivity. At various stages in our lives we all receive care. It is part of the human condition. There is currently no adequate and acceptable word for someone receiving care, just a variety of awkward terms such as 'person being cared for', 'loved one', etc. To make this book easier to read, I will use a few simple terms throughout to refer to the person receiving care. Since the book focuses on care of older people, and since most carers for older people are family members, I mainly use the terms 'the older person' or 'your relative' to refer to the person being cared for. This is also intended to cover the equally important situation where friends are providing care. When discussing a general point, I use the term 'care recipient' if suitable in the context.

I use the term 'family carer' to refer to a family member or friend providing regular unpaid care, although people receiving Carer's Allowance or Carer's Benefit are also included in this definition. I use the term 'care worker' to describe professional, paid care workers, whether employed by the HSE, agencies or families.

There is a stage of ageing during which a person may enter a period of 'terminal decline'. This is not an exact medical term, but it can be understood as a period when the older person becomes more frail and dependent on a continuous basis. Sometimes the term 'progressive dwindling' is used to mean much the same thing. In medical terms it can be called 'systems failure', where the body's systems and organs have started to fail. Such failure can be very short or may last several months. The older person may appear to 'recover' to some extent at times, but the next time they 'go down', they may deteriorate further than before. This stage may occur after a period of hospitalisation or may start with a noticeable increase in dependency. This is the end-of-life period for the older person, and is a particularly difficult time for carers. The term 'terminal decline' is used in various places throughout this book to discuss issues of particular relevance to carers of people at end of life.

I also use the commonly known term 'the Fair Deal' to describe the current Nursing Homes Support Scheme (NHSS).

HOW TO USE THIS BOOK

The book is intended as a 'dip-in' book – it can be read in sections as the need arises. Parts I and II provide an overview of caring for an older person, and the subsequent sections deal with particular aspects of caring and can be read independently. Two key methods are used to make this book a practical reference that can be consulted as necessary:

- Checklists and templates, such as the 'Am I already caring?' check-list, will help you to apply the information in this book to your own situation.
- 'Where to get this help' boxes indicate exactly how to access available resources, and who should be approached for a particular form of help.

There is also detailed guidance on filling out the Fair Deal forms and applying for the various grants that are available from local authorities (Chapter 11).

In discussing family caring, the metaphor of adults on planes putting on their own oxygen masks before helping children with theirs is often used. Put simply, this book emphasises again and again the need for carers to take care of themselves and for society to take care of carers. Today's demographic – a rapidly ageing population of individuals living longer with poorer health – has existed only for a couple of decades. Studies across the world have proven beyond doubt that caring has negative effects on carers' health. Nobody knows for sure what the long-term outcome will be, but without doubt, a carer who becomes seriously ill cannot care for anybody. Statistically, today's younger carers (those in their 30s, 40s and 50s) have decades to live. For society to neglect the health and wellbeing of carers now is to pile up problems for the future, problems that may culminate in today's carers themselves needing care for longer than they should. This pushing of healthcare costs downstream needs examination.[7] The work and needs of carers have, until recently, gone relatively unnoticed. This book takes the view that supporting older people is inextricably intertwined with supporting their family carers; it views the older person and their family carers as a unit, so that neglect of one will adversely affect the other. While there is still time, we need to review the current system and understand where it is working and where it is failing, learn from best practice in other countries, and create and implement a fair and easy-to-access national system of support for older people and their family carers. This process has been started, and now is the optimum time to ensure the best possible outcome. Until such time as

---

[7]   Freedman, David H., 'Health Care's "Upstream" Conundrum', *Politico*, 10 January 2018, available from: https://www.politico.com/agenda/story/2018/01/10/long-term-health-nation-problems-000613/.

this system exists, it is hoped that this book will provide some assistance to carers under pressure.

Finally, while every effort has been made to ensure that the information in this book is correct and up to date, there is a possibility of errors. If you would like to raise any such error, please get in touch at: familyguidetocaring@gmail.com.

2

When does caring start?

WHAT IS A CARER?

Many of us believe that a carer is someone who lives with a person who needs help with the general activities of living and who provides almost full-time assistance. There are, indeed, many carers who can be described in these terms. However, anyone who provides care, even part-time, on a regular basis to another person is a carer. As discussed in the Introduction, the term 'family carer' will be used to describe any family member or friend who provides regular, unpaid care to an older person.

The *Oxford English Dictionary* defines the word 'carer' very simply as: 'A family member who regularly looks after a child or a sick, elderly, or disabled person.' The UK organisation Carers Trust gives this definition: 'A carer is anyone who cares, unpaid, for a friend or family member who due to illness, disability, a mental health problem or an addiction cannot cope without their support.'

Census 2016 defined a carer as someone who 'provides regular, unpaid personal help for a friend or family member with a long-term illness, health problem or disability (including problems which are due to old age). Personal help includes help with basic tasks such as feeding and dressing.' The National Carers' Strategy, the strategy for family carers published by the government in 2012, defines a carer in this way: 'A carer is someone who is providing an ongoing significant level of care to a person who is in need of that care in the home due to illness or disability or frailty.'

From these definitions it is clear that the essential elements defining family carers (as opposed to paid care workers) are:

- The personal connection (care is for a family member or friend)
- The care is regular
- The care is unpaid (although family members providing full-time care and receiving Carer's Benefit or Allowance are also considered family carers)

This is the type of care that we naturally expect in family relationships.

HOW MANY FAMILY CARERS ARE THERE IN IRELAND?

The Introduction to the National Carers' Strategy 2012 states:

It is expected that Ireland's ageing population and medical advances in relation to disability and chronic illness will result in more people with longer-term and complex care needs requiring care and being cared for in the community in the future. At the same time ... social trends ... may have implications for the number of people that will be available to assume these caring responsibilities.

The Census of Ireland 2016 found that 4.1 per cent of the population or approximately 195,000 people reported providing unpaid care. The Central Statistics Office's (CSO) 2015 health survey suggests a figure of 360,000 family carers. More recently, Care Alliance Ireland, the national network of voluntary organisations supporting family carers, has calculated that around 391,000 people in Ireland are family carers – around one in ten.

Figure 2.1: One in ten people in Ireland is a family carer

Source: Central Statistics Office, 2016

One reason for the lower census figure may be that part-time carers often don't regard themselves as carers. However, a major study in 2014[8] found that 'the majority of carers provide between one and fourteen hours of care per week.' The number of hours of caring can, therefore, vary widely, from an hour or two a couple of days per week to full-time. It is important to remember that, whatever the level of care, anyone engaged in helping another person regularly is a carer.

These figures cover all carers including carers of children and young people with a disability. In terms of older people, in 2014 it was estimated that there were 164,000 people over 50 who required help with some of the activities of daily living (defined as everyday self-care activities such as washing, grooming and eating; Chapter 3 will explore these in more detail). Some of these 164,000 people may have been receiving care from professional care workers only, but most no doubt also had family carers, perhaps more than one. This gives an idea of the numbers providing family care for older people in Ireland today.

---

[8]   Lafferty, A. Fealy, G. Downes, C. and Drennan, J. (2014) *Family Carers of Older People: Results of a National Survey of Stress, Conflict and Coping.* Dublin: NCPOP, University College Dublin.

The Alzheimer Society of Ireland[9] gives figures for dementia sufferers and their carers, based on Census 2011:

- It is estimated that the number of people living with dementia will rise to 153,157 by 2046 due to population ageing.
- There are approximately 50,000 family carers caring for someone with dementia.
- For each person diagnosed with dementia there are at least three family members directly affected.

Read more

- Central Statistics Office, Health Survey 2015: http://www.cso.ie/en/releasesandpublications/ep/p-ihs/irishhealthsurvey2015/

WHO CARES?

As we noted, the 2016 Census found that 4.1 per cent of the population identified themselves as carers, an increase of just over 4 per cent from 2011. Of these, 60.5 per cent were women and 39.5 per cent were men. Over half of carers were between the ages of 40 and 59. Another assessment of carer numbers[10] found that 64 per cent of carers were women, and that 32 per cent worked full-time in employment.

In 2017, Care Alliance Ireland published a paper defining and profiling family carers in Ireland. The authors said: 'When asked to imagine a typical "family carer" in the Western world, most people think of a woman in her 40s or 50s caring for her elderly parents. ... [T]he ... people most likely to be carers in Ireland are, indeed, mid-life women (nearly 10% of all women aged 45–49 are providing care).'

Census after census, study after study, women emerge as more likely than men to be carers. Current estimates are that women undertake between 60 per cent and 70 per cent of caring in Ireland. Until quite recently, care of older people was in general adequately managed by families. The period of intensive caring tended to be shorter than it is today, while the fact that

---

[9] www.alzheimer.ie
[10] Quarterly National Household Survey 2009.

many women were not employed outside the home meant that there was a ready pool of family carers. In addition, larger families meant that caring duties could be shared more widely. A recent study[11] looked at the particular issue of women as 'sandwich carers':

> [Home care] is a particularly pertinent issue for women who have traditionally been the main carers. As the educational attainment and labour force participation of women has increased, so too the average age of starting a family has extended. This has the effect of creating the 'sandwich generation' where women are raising a family and providing informal care simultaneously. Such a model is not sustainable and supplementing informal care may be a way forward.

The number of men caring is growing, however, with just over 39 per cent of carers identified in the 2016 Census as male. Research indicates that men are less likely to publicly identify as carers, or to take part in support groups. An article in the *Irish Examiner* in August 2013[12] put it this way:

> Many men ... do not seek support, because this may be perceived as a public acknowledgement of their vulnerability and ultimately, an admission of failure. These problems are further compounded by the fact that caring has traditionally been seen as something that women do.

There are also 'young carers', defined variously as people under the age of nineteen years or under fifteen years. Census 2016 found that 3,800 carers were aged under fifteen years, and many of these were involved in the care of siblings, although others were caring for adults.

The most likely primary carer of a person over the age of 50 is the spouse of the care recipient.

It is clear that the social, medical and demographic changes of the last two or three decades mean that the care of older people will, in the near future, be a significant issue for almost all of us, either as caregivers or

---

[11]   Hanley, P. and Sheerin, C. (2017) 'Valuing Informal Care in Ireland: Beyond the Traditional Production Boundary', *Economic and Social Review*, 48(3): 337–364.

[12]   'Male Carers Ireland's Unsung Heroes', *Irish Examiner*, 29 August 2013, available from: https://www.irishexaminer.com/farming/arid-20241296.html.

recipients of care. Studies show that societal changes such as those listed below have significantly increased the amount of care required and reduced the pool of available family carers:

- Women taking part in the workforce, with often both parties in a couple working or having to work outside the home
- Smaller families
- The general ageing of the population
- Medical advances which have meant that people are living longer with chronic health problems
- More people over the age of 80
- Rising dementia figures

As discussed previously, in the near future the answer to the question 'Who cares?' is likely to be 'All of us'.

WHAT DOES A CARING SITUATION FOR AN OLDER PERSON LOOK LIKE?

There is no typical caring situation, although there are patterns. Some people, through whatever combination of life circumstances, are unfortunate enough to have few family members or friends available to look after them as they age. Some very old people may have outlived most of their family and friends. Some people have children who live abroad or too far away to provide regular help. Some have a partner or spouse to care for them, and some also have children and other relatives, perhaps nieces, nephews or grandchildren. Some have good friends to help out. Although there are no official terms for the various types of carers, the following sections attempt to describe in brief the main 'types' and groupings of carers, and the particular problems each may face.

Primary carers and 'secondary' carers

The loose term 'primary carer' is used to describe the person who is the main carer for the older person, usually the person who lives with the older person. This is most often the spouse of the older person. There is currently no term in use for the 'helper carers', often the adult children, who assist the primary

Figure 2.2: Analysis of Ireland's carers 2019

Family Carers in Ireland

Guiding support for family carers

Who Is a Carer?
Someone who provides regular, unpaid personal help for a friend or family member with a long-term illness, health problem or disability (CSO, 2016)

Who Cares?
360,000 or **10%** of the adult population (CSO, 2016)

What's the Kinship Between Them?
86% of Family Carers are Family Members. Most are caring for an ageing parent or a child with high support needs. (CSO, 2016)

How Much Care Is Provided?
Average of **44.6 hours** care provided per week (CSO, 2016)

How Do We Financially Support Full-time Family Carers?
75,000 carers receive the Carers Allowance
Over **100,000** receive the Annual Carer Support Grant (DSP, 2017)

Is the Role Challenging?
50% of carers have had the experience of being mentally and physically 'drained' by their caring role (CAI/ICP, 2009)

What Are the Drivers of Ill Health in Caring?
Dealing with verbal/emotional abuse; Coping with bizarre/inconsistent behaviour; Getting up in the night. (CAI/ICP, 2009)

What Is the Health Impact?
Over **half** reported having a medical problem, the most frequent being back injury, and over half also reported having a significant mental health problem, the most frequent being anxiety disorder. Most carers stated that they had **no time for themselves** and worried how the person they cared for would cope if they had to stop caregiving due to illness or death. (CAI/ICP, 2009)

Are Carers Stressed?
27% of carers scored seven or higher on the Caregiver Strain Index (CSO, 2016)

What's the Gender Mix?
Females provide around two-thirds (66.1%) of all care hours, increasing to approximately seven in ten from age 50. But 40% of Family Carers are male. (CSO, 2016)

Do Children Provide Family Care?
11% of school-age children report providing care (Callaghan, 2016)

What Is Public Expenditure on Home Care in 2017?
c€344m (CAI, 2016)

What Share of the Social Welfare Pie do Family Carers Get?
5.3% Percentage of overall Department of Social Protection Budget spent on Income Supports for Family Carers (CAI, 2017)

Are there More Older Carers?
The number of older carers has increased by over **50%** since 2006 (CSO, 2017)

What Are Sandwich Carers?
Usually caring for young children and parents at the same time. The highest concentration of Caring in our population is in the 40–55 age group (CSO, 2012)

What Is the Financial Contribution of Family Carers?
€10bn per year (CAI, 2017)

Can Family Carers Combine Working and Caring?
A third of Family Carers work full-time (CSO, 2012)

Sources of Information
• Care Alliance Ireland (2017) Trends in Family Caring in Ireland in 2017: Review of Awareness, Self-Identification, Official Surveys and Income Supports.
• Care Alliance Ireland (2016) Analysis of Home Care Supports Funded by the HSE 2008/2016. Allowing for an estimated additional €20m being allocated in 2017.
• Callaghan, M., Keane, E. & Molcho, M. (2016). Short Report – HBSC Ireland: Young Carers in the 2014 HBSC Study.
• Central Statistics Office (2017) Census 2016 Chapter 9, Health, Disability and Caring. Dublin: Stationary Office
• Central Statistics Office (2016) Full Census 2016 Questionnaire
• Central Statistics Office (2012) Census 2011 – Profile 8 – Our Bill of Health. Dublin: Stationery Office.
• Central Statistics Office (2010) Quarterly National Household Survey, Quarter 3 2009: Module on Caring.
• Carers Association of Ireland and the Irish College of Psychiatrists (CAI/ICP) (2009) The Health of the Carer in Ireland Survey.
• Central Statistics Office (2016a) Irish Health Survey 2015.   • Family Carers Ireland (2017) 2018 Pre-Budget Submission.
• Health Service Executive (2017) Social Care Operational Plan 2017   • Social Protection, Department of (2017) Ministerial Briefing June 2017.

Source: Care Alliance Ireland

carer. The term 'secondary carer' is used here to describe this network of family and perhaps friends who provide ongoing care, even though they may not live with the older person. A common care situation would be that a spouse/partner is the primary carer, while the adult children act as secondary carers, as shown in Figure 2.3. A point to note here is that the primary carer may themselves be receiving some care from the secondary carers, meaning that in effect the primary carer is also a care recipient.

Figure 2.3: Primary and secondary carers

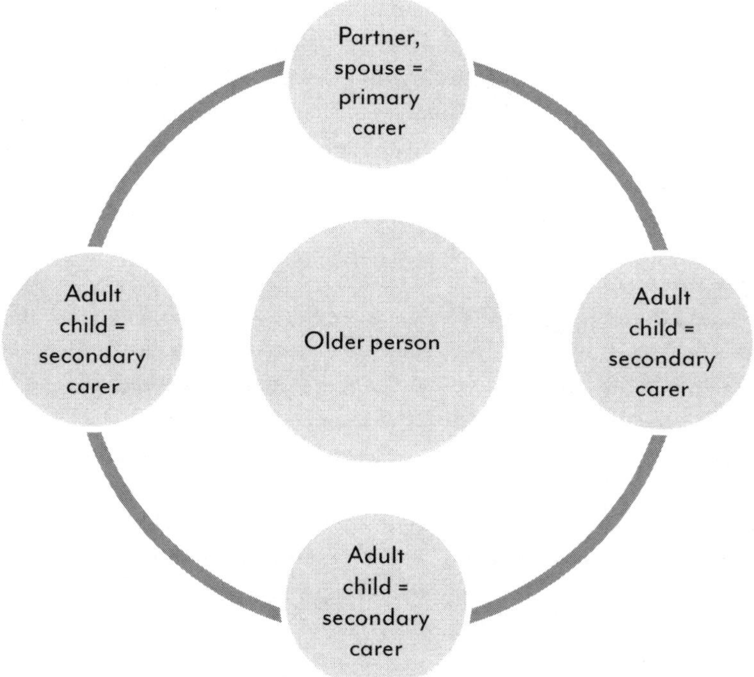

Older carers who themselves need care

As noted above, some older carers themselves need care. They are likely to be providing care by their presence in the home, by coordinating care workers coming to the house, and by looking after many of the day-to-day needs of the older person, such as providing meals. However, the 'secondary' carers (usually adult children) may be managing aspects of the care of both the care recipient and their spouse. Common tasks include dealing with finances, managing maintenance of the house, hiring or supervising care workers, dealing with medical appointments and managing medication.

Full-time and part-time carers
As discussed above, many people think of a carer as someone who lives with an older person and provides round-the-clock care. We often think of someone giving up their job to take on the role. This indeed can be the situation for a full-time carer. Most full-time carers are spouses, partners or adult children of the person needing care. Full-time carers may be entitled to state support payments such as Carer's Allowance/Benefit, and the Carer's Leave Act 2001 grants the right to take unpaid leave from employment to care for a person in need of care (discussed in Chapter 11). As noted, however, the majority of family carers are part-time carers, with the biggest proportion providing care for between one and fourteen hours per week. Families often manage care by establishing a rota in which a number of family members take part.

Lone carers
Census 2011 found that 40 per cent of carers were the sole carer for their relative. This group has a particular set of issues, of which the main one is the propensity for isolation. The risk of isolation is most pronounced for rural carers and those who cannot leave their relative alone. This group is in great need of adequate state-provided home care hours to allow them to leave the house, and respite (where the older person is looked after by others for a period) to allow them to regain their strength and gather their resources. This group may also benefit most from contact with other carers and participation in carer community groups, so that they can ask questions and learn from the experiences of others.

Sandwich carers
The term 'sandwich carers' is used for people who have care responsibilities for both children and elderly parents or other relatives at the same time. Some may also be in employment. They may experience feelings of guilt on a regular basis, because they feel pulled between their various responsibilities and so worry that they are not doing anything particularly well. Time pressure is a particular issue for this group, and they are especially likely to

be at risk of compassion fatigue (see Chapter 16) because of the multiplicity of claims on their energy and resources.

Carers with health problems

As will be discussed throughout this book, research has confirmed beyond doubt that caring takes a toll on the physical and mental health of carers. Back problems, anxiety and depression are common. The extent of this 'cost of caring' depends on each individual's set of circumstances, but it is clear that a significant number of carers themselves experience health problems.

SIGNS THAT HELP IS NEEDED

The realisation that an older person is at the stage of needing help is gradual, both for the older person themselves and for the family. The family may realise that a caring situation has arisen while the older person may still deny that they need any care. People who have lived full, independent lives will not readily relinquish control over any aspect of their lives to others. This is a difficult issue, because the demands on the family carers may be high while the person being cared for may constantly deny that the care is happening and that they need care. This kind of resistance to help will be discussed further in Chapter 2.

Everybody is different, but some of the signs that a person is 'slowing down' are common. The list below presents some of the most common signs.

Self-care and grooming
- Being less well-presented than usual: perhaps having the odd stain on clothing, forgetting to put on lipstick, wearing the same clothes over a number of days, appearing with unbrushed hair

Forgetfulness
- Repeating requests
- Repeating stories, perhaps even a number of times in the same conversation
- Forgetting dentist/doctor/hospital/optician appointments
- Losing things – regular items include keys, phones and glasses

- Forgetting to deal with paperwork or pay bills (A particular concern here is that car, house and health insurance are kept up, as it is not unknown for insurance to lapse simply because the older person can no longer deal with correspondence.)

Mobility and driving
- Asking to be brought to or collected from appointments when this has not been a problem in the past
- Walking more slowly
- Walking less than usual
- Complaining of pain when moving or walking
- Finding it difficult to bend to pick up items that have fallen
- Experiencing 'bumps' when driving, such as denting their own or others' cars when parking
- Avoiding places where parking is difficult

Loss of confidence
- Avoiding social situations that they have previously enjoyed
- Driving less often or restricting themselves to shorter distances or familiar places
- Showing reluctance to go to crowded or noisy places
- Refusing invitations

Difficulty managing housework and cooking
- Finding it difficult to keep the house as clean and cared for as previously
- Not having sufficient food in the house
- Having out-of-date food in the fridge and cupboards
- Eating less
- Cooking less often and instead eating toast or other easily prepared foods

Other
- Expressing anxiety about various situations or events that have not previously been a problem, e.g. bringing the car for the National Car Test (NCT), booking appointments, etc.

Checklist 2.1 can be used to see if any of these issues apply to your relative.

Checklist 2.1: Does my relative need care?

Self-care/presentation	Y/N
Is my relative sometimes less well-presented than usual, with signs of stains on clothing?	
Do they forget to shave or put on lipstick, in a way which is unlike them?	
Do they wear the same clothes for too many days?	
Do they forget to brush their hair?	
Do they wear clothing suitable for the weather?	
Do they exhibit other signs of forgetfulness in relation to self-care, such as forgetting to put on socks or to bring a coat?	
Forgetfulness	
Do they repeat requests or stories?	
Do they forget appointments?	
Do they often lose things at home?	
Do they neglect paperwork or bills?	
Mobility	
Do they ask to be brought to or be collected from appointments?	
Do they walk more slowly than they used to?	
Do they walk less than usual?	
Do they complain of pain when moving or walking?	
Do they find it difficult to bend to pick up items that have fallen?	
Do they avoid social situations that they have previously enjoyed?	
Do they drive less often or restrict themselves to familiar places?	
Do they show reluctance to go to crowded or noisy places?	
Do they refuse invitations they would previously have accepted?	
Have they had 'bumps' when driving or parking?	

Managing housework and cooking	
Can they plan, buy and cook meals?	
Are they eating enough and eating healthily?	
Is the housework slipping?	
Maintaining the home	
Are they able to manage repairs to the house, book a boiler service, etc.?	
Managing finances	
Can they still manage their finances?	
Is paperwork building up?	
Do they ask for letters to be explained?	
Are bills being paid or are overdue notices being received?	
Is insurance being maintained?	

How do you start to 'care'?

There isn't a day on which you wake up and realise you are a 'carer' and that your parent or relative needs care. The process is ever-evolving; indeed, the constantly changing situation is a major challenge for families. When you begin to notice some of the signs discussed in the previous section, you might visit or ring your relative more often, either to reassure them or yourself. The next stage might be bringing them to a medical or hospital appointment. Perhaps they will ask you to fetch an item for them that they cannot get themselves, and maybe this involves a trip to town. You might start inviting them to dinner once or twice a week, both to make sure they are eating well and to provide company. You might encourage them to hire a cleaner. These changes are possibly the beginning of a process. There is nothing unusual about any of them; they are normal ways we help older or less able people. But they may indicate the start of something.

Are you already caring?

Sometimes we are already caring before we put a name to it, because providing care for loved ones is a completely natural thing, and is a continuum from such normal family activities as phoning and cooking meals for someone, to providing full-time care in all aspects of their life. Checklist 2.2 will allow you to see what you already manage for your older relative. If you answer 'yes' more than once or twice, then you are already a carer.

Figure 2.4: Common caring tasks

Checklist 2.2: What care do I already provide?

Care activity	Y/N
Do I visit or ring my relative more often than I used to?	
If I ring/visit more often, is this to reassure my relative or myself, or both of us?	
Has my relative asked me to bring them to hospital or other appointments?	

Have I brought my relative to appointments?	
Have I had to find or buy items for my relative because they cannot do this themselves?	
Have I started to invite them to dinner more often?	
If so, is this because I want to make sure they are eating well?	
Is it because they need company?	
Have I hired/found a cleaner for my relative?	
Have I hired/found a gardener or other help for tasks they could previously manage alone?	
Do I fill their freezer with dinners?	
Do I do their shopping online?	
Do I buy clothes or other personal items for them?	
Do I carry out cleaning or other household tasks when I visit?	
Do I help them to manage their paperwork and finances?	
Do I help them to manage their medication?	

CARING THAT STARTS AFTER A HOSPITAL STAY

Of course, it is also possible that an older person will have some sort of illness or accident resulting in a hospital stay, and following discharge they will need some sort of help at home. This is another way in which a family may experience the start of caring. In some ways there will be more direction if this happens, as often the care plan for discharge from hospital will involve referral to the local public health nurse (PHN). The discharge plan may involve care workers calling to get your relative up in the morning and help them to bed at night, or the older person may have been referred for ongoing physiotherapy or occupational therapy. Table 2.1 shows health professionals who may be involved in your relative's care after discharge from hospital.

It may be much more obvious after a hospital stay that some form of extra help is needed than when there's a gradual loss of independence. For example, the person may need help with dressing for some time, or help with cooking or housework.

Table 2.1: People who might be involved in your relative's care after a hospital stay

Person	Organisation
General practitioner (GP)	Local doctor's surgery
Consultant	Discharging hospital (for reviews)
Public social worker	HSE
Public health nurse	HSE
Physiotherapist	HSE/private
Occupational therapist	HSE/private
Speech therapist	HSE/private
Dietician	HSE/private
Care workers/home helps providing 'care hours'	Either provided by the HSE or paid for privately

3

The conflict between wants and needs

THE PERSON

The individual who starts to lose independence and needs the help of others is first and foremost a person. What is a person? There is no easy answer. A simple definition of a person is: 'A human being regarded as an individual.' When we consider what makes up a person, the following might come to mind:

- Personality
- Life experience
- Values and beliefs
- Occupation
- Hobbies

- Physical attributes
- Ethnic background or cultural beliefs

Your relative might have had important roles in their working life. They may have been an accomplished musician, an innovative scientist, an inspirational teacher. They may have been like most of us: ordinary, independent, hard-working and capable. They are likely to have looked after others at various stages, whether their own parents, their children, other relatives or friends. They have personalities, quirks, likes and dislikes. They know how they like their coffee, what detergent they prefer, which way they want their furniture arranged. They make their own decisions about what they do and where they go. They are unique individuals, with a lifetime of learning and experience behind them. What they *want* is to continue to be independent. What they *need* is help in the areas they find difficult. The problem is that many people will fiercely resist loss of independence.

GRADUAL LOSS OF INDEPENDENCE AND HOW IT IS MEASURED

As discussed in Chapter 1, the caring experience of a family is not static, but an evolving state. It involves stages of realisation for both the older person and family members. Different family members may have different views on what help is needed; some may feel a higher level of care is required than others do. The person needing care may not recognise, or may not want to admit, that they need help. They may fiercely resist every attempt to help. What they want and what they need may be in direct opposition.

All of us have basic common needs, such as the need for food, warmth, shelter and medical care. Someone who is becoming frail may have problems dealing with even these basic needs. As discussed above, they may have difficulty shopping, preparing meals, attending medical appointments, keeping their home clean and ensuring they have heating fuel. They may neglect household repairs and forget to pay bills. They may have difficulty keeping on top of the laundry and attending to personal care. They may also be lonely.

In summary, common areas where help might be needed include:

- Getting about

- Household tasks
- Meal preparation
- Personal care
- Companionship

Instrumental activities of daily living

One difficulty for families is that loss of independence is slow and gradual. As we have seen, the first signs, such as repeating questions or forgetting information, may not be recognised by anyone. To help to identify patterns in such small and ordinary difficulties, health professionals use the concept of 'instrumental activities of daily living' (IADLs), and it can be very useful for families to have a general understanding of this concept. Instrumental activities of daily living are simply the tasks and activities we do every day – tasks that are necessary for a person to live independently within the community without help from another person. Having a general understanding of these can help family members to establish which type of support their relative needs. The instrumental activities of daily living include:

Cleaning and home maintenance This includes keeping living areas clean and managing home repairs, booking services, etc.

Shopping for groceries and other necessities and preparing meals This includes buying clothes and cleaning supplies, etc.

Managing medication This includes obtaining prescribed medication and making sure it's taken correctly.

Managing money and finances This includes paying bills and dealing with taxes and other financial tasks.

Moving within the community This can be by driving or by organising other forms of transport.

Managing communication by using the telephone, email, etc.

In general, a person must be able to perform both the *instrumental* activities of daily living and the 'activities of daily living' (ADLs) (described in the next section) in order to live independently. Help is needed where there are gaps in these abilities.

Activities of daily living

The second main concept used by health professionals to measure declining independence is the activities of daily living (ADLs). These are everyday self-care activities that are necessary for healthy functioning. The basic ADLs are:

- Bathing and showering
- Personal hygiene and grooming, including managing hair
- Dressing
- Toilet hygiene
- Functional mobility – moving around
- Self-feeding, not including cooking

When function begins to be lost, the usual pattern is: 1) hygiene, 2) mobility and toilet hygiene, and 3) eating.

Levels of dependence

As loss of function is a continuum – starting from a low level of loss in one or two areas, and progressing for some people to significant levels of dependence in most areas – it is helpful for family members to be able to evaluate at some level the progression of loss, as help will need to be provided or increased in the areas affected. It is useful to be clear on the signs so that help can be increased as necessary, rather than the situation being a continuous exercise in firefighting.

Health professionals in Ireland calculate a person's level of dependence based on a scale called the Barthel Index, which measures functioning in the activities of daily living. Ten variables are measured: bowel continence, bladder continence, grooming, toilet use, feeding, transfer (e.g. moving from chair to bed), mobility, dressing, stairs, bathing.

Each variable is given a score from zero to three (with zero being the lowest level of ability and three the highest). The possible outcomes are: 'independent', 'needs some help', 'needs help', etc. Scoring is as follows:

- 16–19 indicates low dependency
- 11–15 indicates medium dependency

- 6–10 indicates high dependency
- 0–5 indicates maximum dependency

MORE EXTENSIVE NEEDS

A person with a specific medical condition or disability will have extra care needs, commonly including:

- Managing medical supplies, perhaps including continence supplies
- Obtaining and maintaining specialised equipment, such as a wheelchair, frame, medical bed, hoist, etc.
- Making and attending medical appointments
- Following the instructions of a physiotherapist, speech therapist or other health professional
- Managing a special diet, for example, for diabetes or difficulty swallowing

In these circumstances the family carer will have a lot of interaction with medical professionals, the local pharmacy, the public health centre and the person's GP. All of these require significant carer input. For example, ordering, collecting, administering and keeping track of medication is a significant task in itself.

Communication

Another loss experienced with age is the ability to communicate, which can obviously present particular challenges for carers. A person's ability to communicate can be assessed on five levels:

- No problems
- Retains most information and can indicate needs verbally
- Difficulty speaking but retains information and indicates needs non-verbally
- Can speak but cannot indicate needs or retain information
- No effective means of communication

Source: HSE Common Summary Assessment Report

Again, difficulty communicating will indicate a need for help in that area. Managing impaired communication is dealt with in Chapter 7.

Other risk factors

Other risk factors taken into account when assessing levels of dependence include:

- Pressure sore risk (for those confined to bed/wheelchair)
- Falls risk
- Nutritional risk
- Wandering risk
- Mental health problems

There are also social risk factors such as isolation.

Cognitive decline

A test for loss of cognitive function extensively used in the Irish health services is the Mini Mental State Examination (MMSE). This is a 30-point questionnaire designed to test cognitive impairment in different areas. The test includes:

Orientation to time	Awareness of season, year, date, day, time
Orientation to place	Awareness of location from country to own address
Registration	Repeating prompt words
Attention and calculation	Counting backwards from 100 in sevens, or spelling a word backwards
Recall	Repeating the previously prompted words
Language	Naming common objects, e.g. a pencil or a watch
Repetition	Speaking a phrase back to the assessor
Complex commands	Can involve drawing a figure/shape but varies

The maximum score is 30, and the results are evaluated as follows:

24–30   No cognitive impairment
18–23   Mild cognitive impairment
0–17   Severe cognitive impairment

Difficulties in particular areas can be identified by this test, and actions can be taken in response.

WHAT THE PERSON WANTS AND WHAT IS POSSIBLE

Now we come full circle – having considered all the ways in which a person may lose independence, we go back to the question: what does the person want? The Irish Longitudinal Study on Ageing (TILDA), carried out by Trinity College Dublin, found that for the majority of older people the answer is to remain at home for as long as possible, and this has been confirmed in other studies.[13] As will be discussed in Chapter 4, keeping people at home for as long as possible is also the focus of the Irish public health system, a key plank of which is the provision of care in the community. This wish to remain at home also ties in with the proposed new statutory home care scheme. Fortunately, public policy and the wishes of older people and the majority of their families are at one in this regard. This book will explore the limits of what is *possible* in a way that gives equal attention to the needs of older people and their family carers. A 2016 report[14] by University College Dublin, Age Action, the Alzheimer Society and the Irish Association of Social Workers acknowledges the tie between the wishes of older people and those of their family carers: 'A difficulty, due to the reliance of the Irish system on family members to provide care, is balancing the older person's preferences and those of family carers.' While very often those preferences coincide, sometimes at least, due to lack of support, the preferences and needs of one or the other will have to yield. In the UK, the Chair of the Standing Commission

13   Donnelly, S. O'Brien, M. Begley, E. and Brennan, J. (2016) 'I'd Prefer to Stay at Home But I Don't Have a Choice', *Meeting Older People's Preference for Care: Policy, But What About Practice?*, Dublin: University College Dublin.

14   Donnelly et al., '*Meeting Older People's Preference For Care: Policy, But What About Practice?*'

on Carers put it like this: 'Historically there has often been too much of a divide between the user and the carer, whereas the physical and emotional well-being of both are inextricably linked.'[15]

In looking at what is possible for family carers of older people, and thus what is impossible, we are moving into relatively untouched territory, in Ireland at least.

---

[15] Russell, P. (2010) 'Introduction', *Carers and Personalisation: Improving Outcomes*, available from: http://static.carers.org/files/carers-and-personalisation-dh-nov-10-5452.pdf.

Part II

A Foundation in Caring and Working with the Public Health System

4

Working with 'the system'

No one can care for an older person alone. This is a point that can't be repeated too many times. No matter how willing and able, no one person can singlehandedly look after all of a frail older person's requirements, from health needs to social needs to financial needs. Caring for an older person can be described as a patchwork or web of care. In the best care system, many people and organisations will be involved, and the main family carer or carers will be the glue holding the web together. The family carers are often in the best position to assess what the older person needs, and the needs will be met by a coalition of healthcare workers, medical professionals, family and friends.

It is important at the outset to realise that help from outside the family may be hugely beneficial to your relative. Older people may have occupied the role of matriarch or patriarch for many years, and be used to holding a position of authority in the family. When it comes to being on the receiving end of requests or instructions from family members, older people may baulk. A simple suggestion, 'Why don't we take a short walk?', may evolve into a battle of wills. The benefit of receiving care from outside the family is that there is no previous relationship to get in the way. A second benefit is that health professionals are trained to handle people, and may be skilled at phrasing suggestions which are for the older person's benefit in a way that is acceptable to them. Realising this can free family carers from some of the guilt they commonly feel at not doing everything themselves.

HOW THE PUBLIC HEALTH SYSTEM IS ORGANISED

Currently, the HSE is divided into four geographical regions – HSE West, HSE South, HSE Dublin North East and HSE Dublin Mid Leinster. Each of these regions is divided into HSE Areas. Area 1, for example, covers Donegal, Sligo/Leitrim/West Cavan, and Cavan/Monaghan.

A major plank of national health policy since 2001 is the implementation of the Primary Care Strategy. This is an approach involving moving health-care away from acute hospitals as much as possible, and providing health services within the community delivered by Primary Care Teams (PCTs). Currently, for example, there are fourteen PCTs in the Cavan/Monaghan HSE Area. Each PCT is responsible for several population areas (towns, villages and rural areas). Figure 4.1 illustrates this organisation.

UNIVERSAL AND MEANS-TESTED CARE

A word now about costs within the Irish public health system. Some health-care is universal, meaning that it is available to everybody, regardless of their financial circumstances. Alternatively, some healthcare is means-tested and people are entitled to services based on income thresholds. Two important means-tested benefits are the medical card and the GP visit card. The main benefits for holders of medical cards are:

- Free GP care
- Free medication (although prescription charges currently apply)
- Hearing and vision checks

- Outpatient and inpatient services in public hospitals
- Aids and appliances to help with mobility difficulties or other disabilities

Medical card holders are also entitled to physiotherapy, occupational therapy, speech therapy, dental and chiropody services; however, there may be waiting lists for some of these services. To avail of any of them, you need to contact private providers in your area (GPs, dentists, chiropodists) who are willing to accept new clients with medical cards, or contact the Local Health Office or public health nurse.

Currently, people over the age of 70 qualify for a medical card if their gross income is not more than €500 a week for a single person and not more than €900 a week for a couple. The GP visit card is now available to everyone aged over 70 without an income test.

A welcome development in 2018 was the granting of GP visit cards to people in receipt of either full or half-rate Carer's Allowance or Carer's Benefit. Carers can apply online at https://mymedicalcard.ie/ or by sending in the application form that is available from Citizens Information Centres or at the web addresses given below.

Where to get this help

- Carer's GP visit card: https://www.hse.ie/eng/cards-schemes/gp-visit-cards/gp-visit-card-for-carers/
- Over 70s medical card or GP visit card: https://www2.hse.ie/services/gp-visit-cards/carers-gp-visit-card.html or LoCall 1890 252 919 to order one in the post. Post the completed form to: The National Medical Card Unit, PO Box 11745, Dublin 11, D11 XKF3.

The HSE's Home Support Service (HSS) (discussed below) is not means-tested but is available to everyone.

THE PRIMARY CARE TEAM AND OLDER PEOPLE

Local public health centres form part of the primary care service delivery. Each primary care team is responsible for looking after the health of people within their area. The primary care team will provide some or all of the following services:

- Nursing
- Occupational therapy
- Physiotherapy
- Psychology
- Speech and language therapy
- Social work
- Dietitian
- Home help
- Day care and respite

One major advantage of the primary care approach for the family carer and the older person is the 'single point of access' – services are generally accessed via the public health nurse, who will arrange for other professionals

Figure 4.1: How the HSE is organised

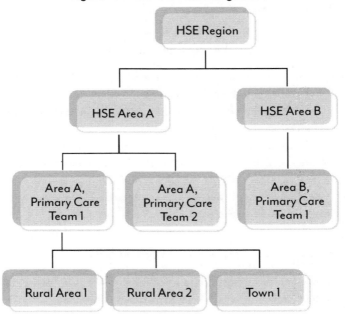

such as physiotherapists to see the older person as needed. This system reduces the burden on the carer to organise all services an older person may need, which may include several of those listed above.

It is important to remember the overarching goal of the public health system as you organise care for your relative – for older people to be cared for at home as far as possible. When you view the situation as one where both the family and health system have a common goal – to keep the care recipient at home – it is easier to work toward achieving this. However, studies have shown that when there is a 'family' providing care it may result in an older person receiving fewer services, so you may become involved in advocacy and negotiation in order to obtain the services your relative and family need. The financial constraints on the health system mean that services are allocated based on need, and a finite amount of funding is available to be divided out. This means, at present, that the help families need will often not be available.

A major part of the policy of keeping people in their homes is the provision of 'home care hours'. These are hours of care that are provided by the HSE, and involve a trained care worker calling to the person's home at agreed times during the day to help with various activities of daily living (see Chapter 3). The help offered can include:

- Getting the person up or getting them ready for bed
- Making breakfast
- Tidying the bedroom and doing light housework
- Providing personal care such as toileting and showering when needed
- Prompting the person to take medication
- Encouraging the person to walk about
- Checking generally that there are no problems, and notifying family if there are

Many professional care workers have completed FETAC Level 5 training modules, although the sector is currently unregulated. It is anticipated that qualifications will be specified when the promised regulation of the home care sector comes through. Care workers funded by the HSE may be employed by the HSE or provided by private agencies. The management at these agencies will support the care workers when problems arise, and liaise with the family. They will work with the family carers, who know the older person best, to draw up a detailed written 'care plan'.

THE HSE HOME SUPPORT SERVICE (HSS)

The public home care system is undergoing reorganisation, with a move away from the previous distinctions between 'home help' and 'home care packages', and toward a single streamlined 'home support' service. As of mid 2019, home care for older people is provided under a HSE scheme called the Home Support Service (HSS). This service replaces the previous Home Help Service and Home Care Package Scheme. Under the old schemes, a distinction was made between three types of home care service, based on the extent of the care provided; see Figure 4.2. The new scheme moves toward one term – home support – for all types of care at home.

Home support is not means-tested and is provided free of charge. Each person is assessed by HSE staff to establish what they need, and support is offered based on this assessment, although budgetary constraints mean that many people are assessed as needing more help than is allocated.[16] Many older people and their families supplement the HSE home support allocation with further home care hours which they pay for themselves.

Although the process of streamlining home care and moving away from the home help and home care package schemes is underway, many people are currently receiving support under these schemes, and so each scheme is described below.

HSE home help

The Home Help Service was the most basic service for older people, and was generally availed of by those with a good level of independence who needed some help with tasks around the house, such as housework, cooking and laundry. While the home help scheme was originally designed to cover household tasks, it evolved to cover personal care such as washing and dressing. Under the Health Acts, the Home Help Service was provided

---

[16] Care Alliance Ireland (2018) *Briefing Paper 2: Public Provision of Home Care in Ireland – Update, October 2018*, available from: http://www.carealliance.ie/userfiles/file/Briefing%20Paper%202%20Web.pdf.

free of charge. Generally, a maximum of five hours per week of home help support was offered if eligibility conditions were met. At the time of writing the situation is changing as the new Home Support Service evolves.

Figure 4.2: The three types of home care traditionally available from the HSE

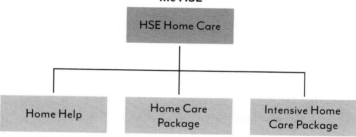

HSE Home Care Package scheme

The Home Care Package (HCP) scheme has been the foundation of the home care system in Ireland and it is not an exaggeration to say that without it many more people would have required long-term nursing home care. Most people understand it as a system of 'home care hours' allocated to help older people remain in their homes, although it also includes a number of other services.

The Department of Health's public consultation on home care services, 'Improving Home Care Services in Ireland: Have Your Say', describes the service as follows:

> Home care packages help people who need a higher level of support to live at home. The services provided in home care packages include more home help hours and can also include nursing and therapies such as speech and language therapy and physiotherapy.

The Home Care Package Scheme was designed to help people with medium or high care needs to stay in their own homes. As well as help with household tasks and personal care, the Home Care Package includes physiotherapy, speech therapy, occupational therapy, respite and other services.

An application under the HCP scheme is often made on discharge from hospital, sometimes coordinated by the public health nurse. If the public health nurse coordinates the application, it is made in consultation with the older person and their family. The application can also be made by the older person themselves or by someone on their behalf. An assessment of care needs is carried out by the HSE, often by the public health nurse. The assessment involves a home visit by a health professional, an assessment of functioning, and a conversation with the older person and their family about what is needed.

A HCP approved by the HSE generally includes some daytime home care hours, and in some areas, weekend hours. Only a few health areas provide night hours, although for many families night cover would be the most welcome type of support. If overnight care is needed, families must cover this themselves or supplement HSE care hours with private hours paid for by the older person or the family. Care hours can be purchased from private agencies, or suitable private carers can be employed for overnight stays. However, the cost of round-the-clock care is beyond most families, and this is one major drawback of the scheme.

Another drawback is the inequitable manner in which it is administered: services under the scheme vary by location, and there is no legal entitlement to support. The statutory home care scheme currently being developed by the Department of Health aims to remove geographical inequalities and put in place a legal entitlement to services.

HSE Intensive Home Care Packages
An Intensive HCP is very similar to a standard HCP except that more care hours are available as well as extra services. A small number of people receive an Intensive HCP – at the time of writing fewer than 300,[17] with an average of 29 hours of care per week.

The Department of Health describes this service as follows:

These packages are provided to people who need very high levels of care. These people could need extra help to be allowed home from hospital or to avoid moving to a nursing home. Intensive home care packages give a level of service that is over and above the services provided as part of a standard Home Care Package.

---

[17]   Care Alliance Ireland. *Public Provision of Home Care in Ireland – Update, October 2018.*

The new Home Support Service

The new Home Support Service aims to streamline the previous services, so that an application is made by an older person for 'home support', and the most appropriate support is allocated based on need. The funding for the various schemes has been merged.[18]

Application is made via the new application form, which can be downloaded from the HSS website (see link below) or obtained from the Local Health Office. Home Support Offices have been set up nationwide to help with applications and to administer the service. An information booklet is also available. The service is free of charge, income is not assessed, and no documents are required when making an application.

Under the new scheme, when home support is allocated, it is provided in one of three ways:

- Care is provided directly by HSE staff carers.
- Care is arranged by the HSE with an approved home care provider.
- Care is arranged by the older person and their carers under the new Consumer Directed Home Support (CDHS) scheme.

Under the new Consumer Directed Home Support scheme, funding is made available to the older person to purchase the type of care that suits them best. The funding must be used for 'home support for personal care and essential household duties, respite care, companionship or other specific services which are essential to them remaining at home and maximising their ability to live as independently as possible.'[19] This gives the older person and their family more choices in relation to care.

---

[18]   https://health.gov.ie/blog/press-release/hse-national-service-plan-2018-increased-supports-for-older-people-and-streamlining-of-home-support-services/

[19]   HSE (2018) *Home Support Service For Older People*, available from: https://www.hse.ie/eng/home-support-services/home-support-services-information-booklet.pdf.

The Care Needs Assessment

When an application for home support is made, the HSE carries out a 'care needs assessment', which is described as follows:

> During the assessment, we will look at your care needs including:
>
> - Your ability to carry out the activities of daily living, i.e. bathing, dressing, shopping and moving around
> - Any medical, health and other support services being provided to you
> - Your family, social and community supports
> - Your wishes and preferences
> - The areas of your life where you need support

Limitations of the current HSS

The HSS, as currently implemented, has a number of problems, many of which are under review in the design of the proposed statutory home care scheme by the Department of Health. The most significant problems currently are:

- Assessment of eligibility varies by Community Health Area.
- Funding varies significantly by area – a 2016 report[20] found a variation from the highest funding per head of population of 65+ years at €691 to the lowest at €456.
- Services vary by area.
- Night cover is provided only in a small number of Community Health Areas, but for some carers night cover is the biggest need.
- Management of the scheme varies significantly by area and the overall management structure is unclear.
- Reviews are intended to be undertaken every three months but in practice this does not appear to happen.

---

[20]   HSE (2017) *Activity & Resource Review: Home Care Services*, available from: http://hdl.handle.net/10147/621444.

The HSE guidelines for the HCP scheme state that the contribution of 'informal' carers, or family carers, toward care of the older person should be 'factored in' when an application for a HCP is assessed:[21]

> The HSE recognises the very significant care being provided by informal carers across the country. Informal Care may be provided by family, friends, and/or neighbours who undertake to support a person at home with or without reward. Such informal care should be factored into the supports available to the applicant for a [Home Care Package].

However, there is little guidance on how such informal care should be factored in, and it is difficult to see how it can be achieved in the current system, since neither the capacity nor the availability of family carers to provide care is measured. It appears that a nebulous concept of a family being 'available' is the basis of this factoring in.

_____

Read more

·   HSS Introduction: https://www.hse.ie/eng/home-support-services/
·   HSS information booklet and application form: https://www.hse.ie/eng/home-support-services/home-support-services-information-booklet.pdf

Where to get this help

·   You can apply for home support through your public health nurse or GP.
·   You can apply in person or on behalf of an older relative by collecting an application form from your Local Health Office, or by downloading the application form at the link below, and sending it to your local HSE Home Support Office (the addresses for each area

_____

[21]   HSE (2010) *National Guidelines & Procedures for Standardised Implementation of the Home Care Packages scheme*, available from: http://lenus.ie/hse/bitstream/10147/120850/1/hcpsguidelines.pdf.

are given on the form): https://www.hse.ie/eng/home-support-services/home-support-services-information-booklet.pdf.

- The Manager of Services for Older Persons (MSOP) at your HSE Local Health Office can assist you.
- You can appeal a decision to the HSE Appeals Officers: https://www.hse.ie/eng/about/qavd/appeals-service/appeals-officers-contact-details/.
- In case of problems, you can contact the Chief Officer of the Community Health Organisation that your Local Health Office is in.
- Overall responsibility for home support lies with the Head of Operations and Service Improvement for Services for Older People (SOP) within the Social Care Division of the HSE acting on behalf of the Director of Social Care.

Figure 4.3: How home care is provided under the new Home Support Service

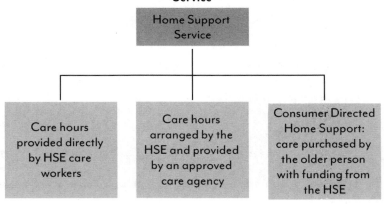

Applying for review of a home care package

When the HCP scheme was set up, it was intended that it would be reviewed every three months; however this does not seem to have happened in practice in many areas. Family carers can apply to have a HCP reviewed if they feel that the older person's needs have increased and that more home care hours are required. If a review is needed, talk to the public health nurse, local Home Support Office or the MSOP at your Local Health Office.

You will need to give definite information about why you think the older person's needs have increased, based on what you have observed. Relevant issues might be increased frailty, difficulty eating, falls, increase in waking at night, etc. At the end-of-life stage, sleeping patterns may become distorted – the older person sleeps a lot during the day but is restless at night. Many carers find it useful to keep a diary in which they record such issues, and professional care workers also log each visit and record any problems. When applying for a review of a HCP, bring these notes with you to back up your application.

Another reason why extra care hours might be needed is if an older spouse/partner who is the primary carer begins to experience loss of function themselves. They may lose confidence after an illness, become forgetful and unable to manage medication, or show reduced mobility and ability to provide care.

While ideally everyone would get the optimum HCP for their needs, services, including home care hours, are dependent on budget constraints, and sometimes there is a waiting list for care services. However, there is a certain amount of informal flexibility within the system, and you need to be tenacious in your approach to seeking services. Family carers know their relative and their relative's needs better than anyone, and have the best insight into the combined capacity of the family to provide care. In making your case, as well as providing definite information on changes observed in the older person, be clear in stating what family members can and cannot do, including what other responsibilities they have. Such responsibilities can include employment, caring for children or teenagers, or caring for other people, such as the parent of a spouse or partner. Obstacles to family care can also include distance from the older person's home, or a carer's own health problems.

In his sensitive and practical guide *Ageing and Caring*,[22] Professor Des O'Neill describes how 'the help and social care response [melts] away when [the health system] senses a caring family'. This is confirmed by a finding of the 2016 report *Meeting Older People's Preference for Care: Policy, but What about Practice?*[23]

---

[22]   O'Neill, D. (2013) *Ageing and Caring*, Dublin: Orpen Press.
[23]   Donnelly et al., *Meeting Older People's Preference for Care: Policy, But What About Practice?*

Family carers were identified as key stakeholders in the care and support of older people; however *social workers reported that routinely older people were less likely to get formal support where an older person had family members providing care.* It was also highlighted that often family carers were not provided with concrete, practical community supports such as HCPs or respite until they reached breaking point [emphasis added].

It is unfair that the mere presence of a 'family' can reduce the care provided by the public health system when no evaluation of the resources of a family is carried out. It is, of course, understandable that where budgets are limited, decisions on distribution must be made in as equitable a fashion as possible. The point is that the capacity of family to provide care must be evaluated before support is denied based on presumptions. The public health system may become involved in a family caring situation relatively late in the day, after a period of years during which family carers have managed low or moderate levels of care. The various health professionals may therefore be unaware of any history of caring within a family. The upshot is that by the time the public health system gets involved – perhaps at or near the end-of-life stage – the family carers may have been caring for years and may already be experiencing negative effects on their wellbeing and the onset of compassion fatigue or burnout.

Figure 4.4: Application for review of home support

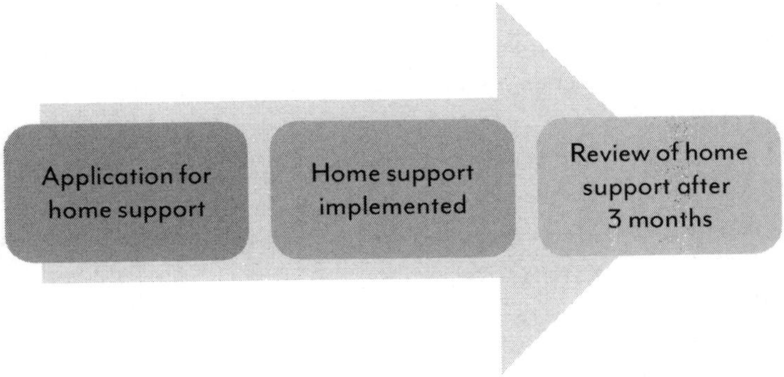

Application for home support → Home support implemented → Review of home support after 3 months

How to make a complaint about the HSS

The HSE offers a number of ways for clients to raise issues with the service:

In person Talk to any member of HSE staff, service manager or complaints office.

Online form Send your complaint securely through the online feedback form which is available on www.hse.ie/eng/services/yourhealthservice/feedback/complaint.

By email Email yoursay@hse.ie with your feedback.

By letter Send a letter or fax to your local Home Support Office. Staff can help you put your complaint in writing, if you require assistance.

By feedback form Complete a feedback form, available at most HSE reception areas, and leave it in the identified areas provided by the local service you are using or visiting. You may also give it to a member of staff or ask them for an address. The form is also available online in 9 languages on www.hse.ie/eng/services/yourhealthservice/feedback/complaint.

Ring us LoCall 1890 424 555: your call will be answered by a staff member from the National Complaints Governance and Learning Team.[24]

HSE DAY CENTRES AND COMMUNITY RESPITE

Day centres

Another support provided by the HSE is day centres, which are located throughout the country and which provide a range of social and therapeutic services to older people. If the older person wants to attend a day centre, the public health nurse or GP can contact a centre on their behalf to enrol them. Transport to the centres is often provided by minibus. Activities vary but tend to run from about 10.00 a.m. to 2.00 p.m. or 3.00 p.m., with tea/coffee and a meal included. If transport is provided, the older person will

---

[24]   HSE (2018) *Home Support Service Information Booklets.*

be collected, dropped off at the centre and brought home afterwards. Day centres particularly benefit people who live alone or those who don't have their own transport. Activities often include exercise classes, sometimes run by professional physiotherapists. Some centres provide newspapers, bingo, singing and other entertainment. Centres run by the HSE may offer occupational therapy and physiotherapy, as well as classes such as art. Other centres are run by voluntary organisations for older people in conjunction with the HSE.

Older people who lack social interaction may benefit in particular from attendance at a day centre. The attendees have time to socialise when not taking part in a class or engaged with a staff member. Some centres offer regular talks on topics relevant to older people, such as safety at home. Some centres offer chiropody, hairdressing and other personal care facilities. Some also provide advice for family carers. Eligibility for attendance at such centres varies by area. Some charge those who can afford to pay a small fee to cover transport and meals.

Where to get this help

- Talk to your relative's GP or public health nurse for further information on local centres and a referral.

Community respite

The respite scheme generally involves the older person moving to a nursing home or community hospital for a period of one or two weeks to allow their carers to have a holiday or a break from caring. Currently, the public health system provides for up to 30 days' respite annually free of charge, generally in a community hospital. A contribution may be required for respite beyond 30 days in a year. This is a very important resource for family carers; indeed, its importance cannot be overstated. For many carers, respite is a chance to regroup. While the older person is being cared for by professional staff, family carers have an opportunity to think, to rest, and perhaps to make some changes or arrangements for the future care of the older person.

Be aware that your relative may, understandably, not wish to move for the respite period, and if the family carers need a break, you may need to try to tactfully bring the older person around to the idea. If they are confused or appear not to understand what is being proposed and why, ask the GP, public health nurse or social worker for advice. However, many older people have good insight into the problems that their family carers face – that they may be finding the role difficult and tiring – and will understand the need for a respite break. You may need to explain the respite option gently in these terms, saying that it will not be for long (a week or possibly two) and that you think it will do everybody good. In an ideal world, respite care would be available in the older person's home, but at the moment such a service does not exist.

Remember too that respite centres will have services available that you might find difficult to access regularly if your relative is confined to the house, such as chiropody and hairdressing. Other benefits may include the older person getting more exercise, as there will be staff available to help with walking (two if necessary). Remember that these are trained staff, used to attending to the needs of older people. There will also often be activities such as art, exercise classes, etc., as well as the opportunity to attend religious services on-site. Since family carers are better carers if they are in good health themselves, respite opportunities should be taken as they become available.

Where to get this help

- Respite of up to 30 days per year is available without charge from the HSE; talk to the public health nurse about organising it.

ENCOURAGING THE OLDER PERSON TO ACCEPT HELP

Even after home support is approved, some older people will resist having home care workers visit them at home, for reasons such as:

- They feel they can manage themselves or with help from family.
- They haven't noticed the care already being provided to them.
- They do not want 'strangers' in their home.
- They resent what they see as interference by the health system.

These are all perfectly understandable, and gentle encouragement may be needed to bring the older person around to the idea of accepting help if their care needs are such that the family cannot provide it all themselves. Patience and tact are needed. Starting small might help – say an hour once or twice per week. Some older people will respond better to the idea that the help is with housekeeping rather than with their own care. You can ask an agency to send the same care worker or workers each time, and they will try to accommodate you. In this way, it is likely that everyone will slowly become familiar with the new situation, and the older person will get to know the care workers. A family member should be present the first few times the care worker calls, to act as ally and advocate, but should take a background role unless called upon, and allow the relationship between the older person and their helper to develop.

FUTURE DEVELOPMENTS AND CHALLENGES IN HOME CARE

As discussed in the introduction, Covid-19 has brought about a sea change in attitudes to care of older people. Most agree that the current model must be redesigned, although how this can best be done is the subject of debate. It is clear that gaps in the current nursing home model failed older people during the pandemic, with lack of state responsibility for residents of nursing homes a key factor. Politicians and others have called for new thinking on care of older people.

Even before the pandemic, however, there were many challenges in the area of care of older people. The Economic and Social Research Institute (ESRI) has estimated that the demand for HCPs will increase by between 44 per cent and 66 per cent by 2030. In 2017 the Department of Health set up a consultation process on the provision of a new statutory home care scheme with three main aims:

1. To provide care needed in the home in an affordable way
2. To ensure that the same care is available no matter where in the country a person lives
3. To regulate all providers of care

Some carer advocates have called for home care funding to work in a similar way to the current Fair Deal nursing home scheme. Under the Fair Deal, nursing home care is co-funded by the state and the older person. A similar scheme for home care means that more people would be able to remain at home for longer, or until the end of their lives, looked after by a team of family members, care workers and health professionals. In November 2017 government officials[25] announced that means-testing was likely to form part of the new statutory home care scheme, and highlighted that during the consultation process, many contributors agreed with the principle of a care recipient contributing to their care. The department said of the new scheme:

> The new scheme will improve access to home care in an affordable and sustainable way. It will provide transparency around service allocation and individuals' eligibility for services, and ensure that the system operates in a consistent and fair manner across the country. The scheme will also result in more effective integration with other health supports including nursing, therapies, and other primary care services. A system of regulation will be designed to ensure public confidence in the standard of the services provided, and to bring Ireland in line with best international practice.

It remains to be seen what effect the scheme will have in practice on older people and family carers. Family carer organisations have argued that co-funding would be considered for a 'fit-for-purpose' scheme but not for a scheme that offers 'the existing, poor quality services'.

Another challenge in the care of older people is demographic changes, such as smaller families, more women in employment and emigration. These have significantly diminished the pool of people available to provide care in a family. The housing crisis has brought new pressures, because for many people, two incomes are now required within a family to afford accommodation, and neither individual may be in a position to take unpaid leave to

---

[25] 'Joint Committee on Health Debate', *Houses of the Oireachtas*, 15 November 2017, available from http://oireachtasdebates.oireachtas.ie/Debates%20Authoring/ DebatesWebPack.nsf/committeetakes/HEJ2017111500002?opendocument #D00100.

care for an older relative. This will mean that gaps in care must be filled by professional care workers. As we discuss in more detail in Chapter 17, the cost of hiring significant amounts of private care is far beyond most families. An older person's savings can be used to fund care, but that person's spouse may themselves need care at a future time, and what will happen to them if the pot is spent? Due to the current situation, nursing home care under the Fair Deal scheme may at some stage be the only practical option, even if nobody wants this and the older person doesn't in fact need nursing care.

The current home care system is also affected by the fact that there are not enough professional home care workers (as opposed to family carers) to fill all the available positions. Agencies that provide home care are constantly recruiting, and the issue is a recurrent news item, both in Ireland and in other countries. Working conditions within the industry are largely responsible for the recruitment difficulties, and people within the industry justifiably lament the low pay (typically about minimum wage), lack of guaranteed hours, unpaid time spent travelling and challenges of the job itself. There is also a lack of recognition of the value of professional care workers, and a lack of respect. Studies have established that poor working conditions promote lower-quality care, and an important aspect of regu-lating the home care sector must involve raising the status of care workers, acknowledging the value of their work, and improving their pay and working conditions.

Migrant workers form a significant grouping within the home care field and it is probably not an overstatement to say that they form the backbone of the home care service in Ireland. A 2017 policy paper[26] notes that: 'In recent years the demographics of care provision have been changing across Europe with a move toward the "outsourcing" of care to migrant carers.' The Migrant Rights Centre stated in 2015[27] that: 'The lack of official data to accurately capture the actual numbers of migrant domestic workers providing home care is a serious gap. This is exacerbated by the fact that a significant proportion of elder care in private homes is informal, undeclared and provided by undocumented migrant workers.'

---

[26]   Hanley and Sheerin (2017) 'Valuing Informal Care in Ireland: Beyond the Tradi-tional Production Boundary'.

[27]   http://www.mrci.ie/wp-content/uploads/2015/09/Migrant-Workers-in-the-Home-Care-Sector-Preparing-for-the-Elder-Boom-in-Ireland.pdf.

Again, the cost of living and the housing crisis may affect the numbers of migrant care workers for whom it is economically viable to continue working in the field in Ireland. The My Fair Home campaign was launched by the Migrant Rights Council of Ireland in 2017 to campaign for employment permits for migrant carers, standardised contracts, regular health and safety checks, compulsory training and compliance with equality and anti-discrimination laws. The 2020 Programme for Government contains a commitment to give long-term undocumented immigrants a route to regularising their status.

The current limited system means that, for people who have high care needs, the cost of buying in private care to supplement state-provided care is prohibitive. When a person needs care at night as well as during the day, the costs involved will exceed the cost of a nursing home. The only secure option at present for most older people with high care needs and their families is to apply for the Nursing Home Support Scheme (Fair Deal). If a person is eligible for the scheme, and their own or the family's funds run out or cannot stretch to private home care, the state will pay the bulk of the cost of a nursing home, with the balance paid by the older person themselves, depending on their income and assets. (For detailed information on the Fair Deal scheme and how to apply for it, see Chapter 9.) The problem is that this reliance on residential care is not in anyone's interests: not those of the older person, the family or the state. The cost to the state of paying for a nursing home is many times the cost of providing home care. One of the three main aims of the proposed new statutory home care scheme is to provide the care needed in the home in an affordable way, and the Department of Health introduced its consultation process on the home care scheme as follows:

> It is widely accepted that most people want to continue to live in their own homes throughout their lives. The Government wants to improve community based services so that people can live with confidence, security and dignity in their own homes for as long as possible. In order to help make this happen, the Department of Health is developing a new scheme that will improve access to the home care services that people need, in an affordable and sustainable way.

As discussed above, medical advances mean that the care situation in Ireland today, and globally, is unprecedented. Despite the admirable objectives of the government's 2012 National Carers' Strategy, the state's approach to family carers has been something of a rear-guard action. It is to be hoped that the proposed new home care scheme and regulation of the home care sector will move toward a national, equitable system of home care for older people that safeguards the health and wellbeing of the unit that is the older person and their family carers.

5

Everyday caring

PRESERVING INDEPENDENCE

As discussed in the Introduction, the concept of caring is a continuum from the normal provision of occasional meals, company, etc. to essentially managing most, or all, aspects of another person's life. It is important to always think in terms of maintaining that person's independence for as long as possible. If someone constantly steps in to do things for them, the older person will soon be unable or unwilling to do things for themselves. While an activity can still be safely undertaken, family carers should encourage the older person to do it. For example, if there is a stairlift in the house, do not constantly offer to get things upstairs – let the older person do it themselves. If they can still cook meals, let them. Encourage them always to do as much as possible for themselves, particularly in relation to personal care. Even when frailty is far advanced, you can hand them a comb to brush their own hair, or give them a razor to shave themselves or a toothbrush to brush their teeth. Encourage them to eat and drink independently for as long as possible. It does not matter how well or badly the activity is carried out – what is important is that it is carried out by the older person themselves. This process of encouragement could be a source of disagreement – some people (young and old) like to have everything done for them, or get into the habit of having everything done for them. But you are doing your relative no favours by constantly stepping in. You are effectively increasing their dependence, and you are showing them you think they are incapable. It is also very important from the perspective of the older person's dignity to help them to maintain the maximum possible independence. Be firm, be encouraging, be tactful – but unless there is a reason for you to take over – don't.

A second aspect of preserving independence is balancing independence against safety. The older person may be prepared to live with the risk of falls or other accidents in order to live more independently. If you are constantly worried about them, you will need to decide between you on an acceptable compromise that gives them maximum independence while allowing you some reassurance. Two possibilities here are Telecare (a system of sensors and alarms that can be installed in a house to notify a carer of falls or other problems; see Chapter 15 for more), or the simple pendant personal alarm (an alarm button worn around the neck or on the wrist that when pressed alerts a monitoring centre; see Chapter 7). In any event, it is important to prevent the cure being worse than the disease – the pursuit of safety should not mean removing the older person's freedom and independence.

HELP WITH GENERAL CARE, HOUSEWORK AND COOKING

Chapter 3 introduced the concept of the instrumental activities of daily living. This is a very useful concept for gauging the amount of help an older person needs. Some older people will have difficulty with only one or two of these activities, while others will need some help with most of them. If the older person has some difficulty, but is to a large extent self-caring, at least in relation to personal care, they will probably not require too many hours of outside care – but they may need companionship, especially if their mobility is limited.

To recap, the instrumental activities of daily living are:

- Cleaning and home maintenance
- Shopping for groceries and other necessities and preparing meals

- Managing medication
- Managing money and finances
- Moving within the community
- Managing communication

If issues with cleaning and home maintenance arise, you can contact the public health nurse to enquire whether your relative can avail of the Home Support Scheme (formerly 'home help'; see Chapter 4). There is no means test for HSE home support. The help is usually provided for a set number of hours per week, and the home support will be allocated on the basis of an assessment by a health professional, often the public health nurse.

Healthy meals

If your relative is no longer able to provide themselves with meals, you will have to make arrangements to do this for them. There are several alternatives here, depending on your own availability and resources and your relative's preferences. A combination of options is often the preferred solution.

Home-cooked meals This is the optimum choice if you have the time and energy to plan, shop and cook. You will know what your relative likes and does not like, and can aim for the optimum diet for their particular needs. The public health nurse can organise a visit from a dietician if necessary. Older adults need more calcium, Vitamin D and fibre than the general population. Information on nutrition for older adults is available from a range of sources, including the HSE and Safe Food.

Read more

- Safe Food: healthy eating for older adults: https://www.safefood.net/family-health/older-adults

---

Meals on Wheels The meals on wheels scheme operates throughout the country, with the help of volunteers. The local health centre or public health nurse will put you in touch with the local manager for the meals on wheels service. The recipient generally pays about €4 per meal, which is usually two courses, but people on low incomes will be accommodated. Talk to the manager before you adopt this scheme to make sure it will suit your relative. There may be no choice of meal, and in some areas the meals are geared toward the old-fashioned meat-and-two-veg type. If your relative does not like this type of meal, or has particular dietary needs, this may not be a good option. However, if your relative is happy with this type of food, then the scheme provides a hot meal every day, with the added benefit of someone calling to drop it in.

Where to get this help

- The public health nurse or GP can give a referral to Meals on Wheels.

Frozen meals All supermarkets have a wide choice of frozen meals that can be stored in a freezer and cooked in the oven or microwaved when needed. Things to look out for include the quality of the meal and the salt, fat and sugar content. If necessary, a small freestanding freezer can provide additional storage to avoid repeated trips to the shops; this may be particularly important if the carer is confined to the house. Another advantage of microwaveable meals is that even if your relative can no longer cook, they may be able to follow the microwaving instructions and thus prepare their own meal. Being able to feed themselves, even to this extent, is an important aspect of preserving independence, as discussed at the beginning of this chapter.

Meals cooked by the home help or other care worker If your relative has home help or you have hired a private care worker, it might be a good idea to ask them to cook meals from time to time for your relative. As older people often prefer small portions, it should be easy to have the helper cook in bulk and divide the meal into portions for the freezer. Although an older person may not be able to cook a full meal, they may be able to heat up a frozen dinner in the oven or microwave and cook a simple accompaniment like potatoes, rice, pasta, salad or vegetables. Again, this option gives scope for prolonging independence. If this situation works for your relative and their home help/care worker, another positive aspect is that the older person might like to help with the meal preparation, giving a sense of involvement.

Meals delivered by private companies Numerous private companies will deliver meals to your door. These will vary in price and quality.

As discussed above, a combination of some of these options may work best, depending on individual circumstances.

HELP WITH PERSONAL CARE

Chapter 3 also introduced the term Activities of Daily Living (ADL), which is the term that health professionals use for everyday self-care activities. ADLs include the following:

- Bathing and showering
- Personal hygiene and grooming (including managing hair)
- Dressing
- Toilet hygiene
- Functional mobility (see below)
- Self-feeding (not including cooking)

As older people become more frail, they may need help with one or more of these activities. The following sections describe the kind of help that you may be able to provide and the kinds of aids and products that are available to help with these activities. Up to December 2019 the Citizens Information Board hosted an excellent website – assistireland.ie – containing a huge amount of information on products and services to help with independent living. The website also had a series of useful articles designed to help older people and their carers to choose the most suitable products for them. Due to resource issues the website no longer exists unfortunately, but there is useful general information on the UK National Health Service website.

Read more

- NHS (UK): https://www.nhs.uk/conditions/social-care-and-support-guide/care-services-equipment-and-care-homes/household-gadgets-and-equipment-to-make-life-easier/

If the older person develops significant mobility difficulties and becomes frail, it is best to have an occupational therapist (OT) do an assessment of their needs. A visit from an OT can be requested via the public health nurse or a private therapist can be engaged. The OT may suggest adaptations that can be made to the house to help the older person and their carers with various activities such as washing and moving around. The OT may provide a detailed specification for stairlifts, ramps, bathrooms, etc. which can be given to a builder or supplier to ensure that the most appropriate equipment is supplied. There are grants available for these types of home adaptations, provided the applicant fulfils the conditions. See Chapter 11 for detailed information on grants available for home adaptations for older people.

Bathing and showering

Keeping in mind the advice above on maintaining independence, try to make it possible for the older person to bath and shower themselves for as long as possible. There are several adaptations that can be made to bathrooms/shower rooms to help with frailty issues. In relation to baths, a bath seat allows the person to sit down while bathing and a good bathmat helps to avoid slipping. A swivel seat allows the user to sit on the seat at the side of the bath and then rotate it over the bath. A shower seat will allow independent showering for longer, as one of the problems with frailty is that the person becomes tired easily. A dropdown shower seat can be attached to the wall and lowered when needed; this type may be useful when other people are also using the shower. Level-access shower cubicles allow the user to walk in without having to take a step up, and many have half doors so that they can also be used by a carer (the carer stands outside the shower and can reach in to wash hair, etc.).

There are many other products to help with personal care, including toileting. Specialised toilets with washing and drying functions are available, while a bidet bowl can be added to convert a standard toilet into a bidet. Again, independent toileting for as long as possible is an important aspect of preserving independence and dignity. If continence becomes an issue, the older person's GP and public health nurse can advise, and the older person may be referred to a specialist.

Note that where alterations are made to a bathroom, etc. to help a person with reduced function to carry out daily activities, a Value Added Tax (VAT) refund may be given (see Chapter 8 for details of the scheme).

Personal hygiene, grooming and dressing

This category of activities of daily living includes managing hair, shaving, dental hygiene, nail care, laundry, etc. A person with decreased mobility (who cannot bend) for example, will have difficulty with foot care. You may need to bring your relative to a chiropodist, or arrange for one to call to your relative's home at regular intervals. Chiropody costs might be covered under the medical card, although you may need to call in a private chiropodist for home visits. You can check this with the public health nurse or OT. Similarly, you may need to help the older person to shave, cut their hand nails and brush their teeth, but keep in mind the discussion above about helping with rather than performing the task.

If your relative is no longer mobile, you may need to get someone to come to the house to cut their hair, or even buy a hairdresser's scissors and learn to cut it yourself. Again, there are a range of products available, including products to help with washing hair at a sink and even an inflatable shampoo basin for washing hair in bed. There is also a freestanding hairdryer available, and long-handled brushes and combs. There are also products for dental care, manicure/pedicure products and skincare aids available.

Make sure that clothes are changed regularly, and provide a laundry basket that the older person can put their clothes into. Keep an eye on clothes; if the older person loses weight you may need to buy smaller sizes.

Where buttons, zips, etc. become difficult, specially adapted clothing can help (and again this promotes independence). There are a range of aids available to help with putting on socks and stockings. A piece of ribbon or cord can be attached to zips to help with pulling them up, or special zipper pulls can be attached. Shoehorns can help with shoes.

It is important to encourage older people to maintain a good grooming routine, for a number of reasons. Firstly, it is very important for their personal dignity that they feel and are clean and well-groomed. They may not always appreciate this, or be cooperative, but it is important to persevere, within reason. Secondly, it is important for their dignity that they present this appearance to other people. Even if they are not concerned about appearance now, it is quite likely that a younger them would approve of you maintaining their appearance for them. Thirdly, it is important for family and care workers assisting them that the older person is helped to keep clean and well-presented. Again, the emphasis is not on doing everything for your relative, but on helping them as needed. The more they feel they can manage themselves the better.

Where to get this help

- The older person's GP or PHN can help, as can an occupational therapist.
- Chiropody may be available under the medical card scheme, but the call-out fee may not be covered. Tax relief may be available where chiropody is prescribed by a doctor; see http://www.citizensinformation.ie/en/health/health_services/care_in_your_community/chiropody_services.html.

ORGANISING MEDICAL APPOINTMENTS

Your older relative may have many medical appointments but might not be able to attend them alone due to reduced mobility, memory problems or anxiety about the appointments. It may be difficult to keep track of and find time to attend them all, especially if you are caring for more than one person (both parents, for example). This is where being organised is crucial, but it is also one area where it is relatively easy to enlist the help of other family members and even friends. A list such as that shown below can help you to keep track of appointments, and is also a useful way of keeping track of medical issues. One way to enlist help would be – with your relative's agreement – to keep the list on a cupboard in the kitchen or on the fridge, and nudge family members toward signing their names to appointments as they arise.

Figure 5.1: Keeping track of medical appointments and enlisting help

Day	Date	Time	Purpose	Location and physician	Whose appointment	Family member attending
Thursday	6 June 2020	2.30 p.m.	Eye review	Mary Tuohy, Waterford Eye Clinic, 1st floor	Anne (Mum)	Tony
Friday	9 August 2020	11.00 a.m.	Cardiologist	Rory O'Malley, Waterford General Hospital, Outpatients Department	Paul (Dad)	Laura
Tuesday	12 November 2020	9.00 a.m.	Warfarin clinic	Waterford General Hospital, 3rd floor, main building	Paul	Susan

How communities can share the care

We discussed earlier how caring for older people 'takes a village'. As a community, it is time to share the care of older people in Ireland. This can be done in a myriad of small ways, all of which save time and stress for family carers. A particular difficulty for some carers is being unable to leave the older person alone in the house. Another challenge for carers and for older people is isolation. The list below includes suggestions for how communities, businesses and public services can share the care of older people in small but important ways:

Local businesses
- Weekly shopping can be ordered online for delivery. This may have a small cost, but may be worth it in terms of ensuring that supplies are available if you cannot leave the house. Some supermarkets have free delivery for over 65s. The shop's website will store your shopping list so that you can change it from week to week if necessary.
- Cafés could hold informal carers coffee mornings which carers could drop in to without prior arrangement. This could be done very informally, with perhaps a sign in the window and a regular allocated table.

- Local pubs or restaurants offering carvery lunches could offer special rates to family carers and their older relatives, perhaps on a monthly or seasonal basis. This kind of initiative would have the benefit of giving the carer and the older person a regular outing to look forward to.
- Some local councils in the UK run schemes whereby registered carers are offered a range of discounts by local businesses that support the scheme. This could be replicated in local areas by the creation of a recognition card and a scheme that local businesses can sign up to.
- It can be difficult for frail older people to attend hairdressers and podiatry/chiropody services. Call-out hairdressing and chiropody are valuable services that local businesses could make available to carers and their older relatives.
- When tradespeople are needed for a carer's home, it is often an emergency situation. Frail older people cannot manage without heat, light, appliances and water. Tradespeople – plumbers, electricians, washing machine repair staff – could offer priority call-out to older people and their carers. Many already do this.
- Taxi companies should offer a wheelchair-accessible service if possible.

Read more

- Local carer discount scheme: http://www.durhamcarers.info/carerscard

Health services
- The GP:
  - » if you are in a situation where it is difficult to leave the house, the GP's surgery will send the repeat prescription for your relative's monthly medication by post or email to your regular pharmacy.
- The pharmacy:
  - » if the older person's GP sends the prescription directly to the pharmacist, they can get your order ready for collection.
  - » some pharmacists will deliver regular medication, which is particularly useful if it is difficult to leave the house.

Public services

- The Gardaí:

  » if your relative has to sign forms that need to be witnessed by particular people, but is unable to leave the house, the Community Garda in your local station will call to the house to act as a witness. No fee is charged for this.

  » the Community Garda will also be able to advise on security in the home.

The library service

- Some libraries offer a call-out service to people who cannot leave their home. This usually involves a staff member calling to the house with a selection of books/audio books based on the older person's preferences. The library staff can also explain how to use audio books or other read-aloud software. Contact your local library to see what services are available.

- Some libraries are fitted with hearing loops, and some also offer a transit wheelchair.

- Many offer activities such as book and film clubs, knitting groups and choir sessions, with some specifically tailored to an older age group.

- Either the library or another local service could offer free computer training to carers to allow them to learn online and keep in touch if they are housebound.

Post offices

- Post offices could facilitate carers by offering a carer's hour for the collection of carer-related payments, to avoid time spent queuing.

Banks

- Banks are stepping back from a personal service and moving toward online transactions and away from face-to-face interaction. This may suit businesses and the tech-savvy generation but it can cause difficulties for older people. Banks should be aware of the particular needs of older people: how they may require more time, more explanation, help filling in forms. Staff should be trained in ways to sensitively help older people with their banking. Simple courtesies like having a chair available should be standard. In some cases, older people develop a lack of trust in the world and in people in general, and this situation needs careful handling.

Schools

- The Friends of the Elderly organisation runs interesting transition year and Civil, Social and Political Education (CSPE) programmes for students. The aim of the programmes is to give older and younger people time to enjoy each other's company:

The planned activities will give the students a greater apprecia- tion of the values of the elderly, of how life was lived in Ireland during the 30's, 40's and 50's, of what the elderly have achieved and what they are passing on to us. We hope that students will take with them the knowledge that the elderly are good company, that ageing is an integral part of life, and that a life well led should be celebrated.

Source: Friends of the Elderly Schools Programmes

A carer's wish list

Carers who use social media could adopt it as a type of 'wish list'. We discuss in Chapter 15 how friends and extended family may want to be supportive but are unsure how to help, and how some stop calling to the house because they want to give the carer 'space'. Carers could use social media to promote their 'wishes' or needs at a particular time. Say, for example, you live in a rural area and need something picked up in a nearby town. If you put this on your social media wish list, a friend or neighbour might see it and oblige by picking up the item. This approach avoids carers having to constantly ask for help, and enables the extended community to share the care of their older neighbours.

Read more

- *The Carer's Companion, Information and Advice for Family Carers in Ireland from Family Carers Ireland:* https://familycarers.ie/carer-supports/help-advice

----

6

Dealing with medical issues and more complex needs

COMMON MEDICAL ISSUES THAT CAN BE DEALT WITH AT HOME OR BY A GP

Blood-testing at home or by a GP

Many older people take the medication Warfarin to prevent blood clots. Warfarin is often prescribed for people who have had a stroke or heart attack, or for people who have had heart surgery. Since the aim is to control clotting rather than to prevent it completely, people taking Warfarin have frequent blood tests to monitor its effect. The Warfarin dosage is adjusted depending on the measured International Normalised Ratio (INR). Hospital phlebotomy clinics and specialist nurses in GPs' surgeries provide blood-testing. When a person's mobility is reduced, mobile phlebotomy services can be used. These are private companies, often run by phlebotomy nurses. They will call to the house to do a blood test, and deliver the sample to the relevant hospital or laboratory for processing. The results are usually sent by the lab to your relative and their GP, and a new dosage advised if a change is necessary. This service must be paid for privately.

Some GPs provide a blood-testing service at their practices. According to the government, this should be free to medical card holders, but at the time of writing there was controversy over whether GPs were entitled to charge for routine blood tests. It appears that some charge a fee of around €10 and some do not charge at all. Some GPs have stated that while the blood test is free, there is a charge for transport of the sample to the lab.

A newer form of treatment that does not require ongoing blood-testing is becoming more widespread, in the form of drugs called NOACs (novel oral anticoagulants).

The community intervention team

The community intervention team is the HSE's 'specialist, nurse-led health professional team'. It provides services to patients with acute episodes of illness 'who require enhanced services/acute intervention for a defined short period of time'. The community intervention team may receive referrals from GPs, hospitals or other community sources. The services of the team are very useful when frailty makes attending medical appointments difficult or impossible.

The services the community intervention team can provide include:

- Administration of intravenous (IV) antibiotics
- Wound dressing
- Acute anticoagulation management
- Urinary-related care
- Ostomy care
- Medication management
- Enhanced nurse monitoring
- Care of patients with respiratory illnesses

Read more

- HSE Community Intervention Teams: http://www.hse.ie/eng/services/list/3/CITs/

Where to get this help

- The public health nurse or GP can make a referral to the community intervention team if care of the above type is needed.

MEDICAL HISTORY

It is very useful to write a detailed medical history for your relative so you have it to hand in an emergency or if they have to be admitted to hospital. Many older people have great difficulty recounting their medical history, especially if they are ill or confused, and having one to hand will help you, your relative and the health professionals. A sample history is shown below. Create a history that is as detailed as possible, and update it in the event of new medical issues or hospital stays. It is a good idea to keep a photo of the document on a phone or a copy in a bag so that it is available in case of emergency.

Table 6.1: Sample medical history

Mary Kelly medical history

DOB:	1 January 1935
Address:	7 Rose Cottages, Anytown
GP:	Dr AB, Main St, Anytown, tel:

Medical

Condition	Date	Doctor/Consultant/Hospital
Fibromyalgia	ongoing	Dr A, New Street Hospital, tel:
Macular degeneration	ongoing	Dr B, Main Street Eye Clinic, tel:

Osteoporosis	ongoing	GP
Arthritis	ongoing	GP
Broken left wrist	2012	New Street Hospital

Surgeries

Surgery	Date	Hospital	Consultant
Tonsils	1960	New Street Hospital	Not known
Varicose veins	1995	New Street Hospital	Not known
Hip replacement (left)	2011	New Street Hospital	Dr X
Cataract surgery	2015	Main Street Eye Clinic	Dr Y

Medication

Medication	Dosage	Date
Warfarin	x mg	correct June 2020
Calcichew Forte	x mg	correct June 2020

MANAGING MEDICATION

Most older people take several types of medication and many need help to manage it. One practical way of keeping track is to fill a pill box each weekend with the following week's medication. Pill boxes are available from pharmacies, and most have four compartments for each day, labelled morning, noon, evening, bed, or similar. If different care workers come to the house at different times, it is vital to have medication organised in advance. Care workers will prompt the older person to take medication, but cannot actually give the medication. It is up to the family carers to organise medication in the correct dosages.

Keep an up-to-date list of all medications and dosages, as shown in the medical history above. All hospitals and respite centres will need a list of current medications if your relative is admitted to either.

As discussed before, it is useful to have email addresses for the GP and pharmacist. Ask the GP if they can fax or email a prescription directly to the pharmacy if there is an emergency or something is needed unexpectedly.

This will save you a trip to the GP's surgery, which is especially useful if it is difficult for you to leave the house. You can also ask whether your pharmacy will deliver to your home – some will do so for people who have regular prescriptions.

Where to get this help

-   The GP and local pharmacist can help you to manage your relative's medication.

MEDICAL SUPPLIES AND AIDS

As your relative's level of dependency increases, they may need aids for everyday activities such as dressing, washing and eating. The occupational therapist and the public health nurse can advise on products available (see also Chapter 5). Some commonly used aids are listed below. Many will be provided free of charge to medical card holders if recommended by the public health nurse or OT.

For people with very reduced mobility who spend a lot of time in bed, a medical bed may be necessary both to reduce the risk of bedsores and to minimise lifting by carers. Medical beds can be raised and lowered by using a control, allowing a carer or the older person to change the position from sitting to lying down and vice versa, thus reducing the need for a carer to lift. The mattress automatically redistributes pressure to reduce the risk of bedsores and increase comfort. The public health nurse can help to organise one if needed.

Table 6.2: Medical supplies and aids

Activity	Aid	Professional who can advise
Dressing	Specially adapted clothing or footwear; zip puller	Occupational therapist
Walking	Stick(s)	Occupational therapist
	Frame	Occupational therapist
	Walker	Occupational therapist

Mobility	Wheelchair	Occupational therapist
	Powered wheelchair	Occupational therapist
	Mobility scooter	Occupational therapist
Eating	Specially adapted food, e.g. puréed food or thickened liquids for swallowing difficulties	Dietician/GP/public health nurse
	Protein supplements for poor appetite	Dietician/GP/public health nurse
Preparing food	Jar opener	Occupational therapist
	Kitchen utensils with padded handles (for people with arthritis)	Occupational therapist
Hearing	Hearing aid	Hearing specialist
Reading	Magnifying glass/suitable glasses	Optician
	Speaking watch/clock	Generally available
Washing	Shower seat or specially adapted shower (see Chapters 5 and 11)	Occupational therapist
	Grab rails	Occupational therapist
Speaking	Communication chart; alphabet chart	Speech therapist/GP
Other	Grip for picking up items from the floor	Occupational therapist
	Remote control with large buttons	Occupational therapist
	Telephone with large buttons	Occupational therapist
	Lighted grab rails; night lights	Occupational therapist
	Medical bed	Public health nurse
	Floor mat with sensors for people at risk of falls	Occupational therapist/ generally available

The concept of universal design is becoming more widely known as the global population ages. The idea behind universal design is that products, buildings and environments are designed to be easily accessible to everyone: older people, people with disabilities, people without disabilities. Examples in Ireland today include ramps at road crossings which allow wheelchair users to cross the road, and 'kneeling' buses. Increased take-up of this concept in the future may mean that common items become easier to use for a greater number of people.

7

Dealing with particular problems of older people

MOBILITY AND SAFE DRIVING

Mobility is a key aspect of preserving independence, and for many people, especially those in rural areas, continuing to drive may be very important to maintaining independent living. Many people continue to drive until well into their 80s and 90s, although there are extra regulatory requirements for older drivers. Under current rules, people over the age of 70 need a certification of fitness to drive from their doctor in order to apply for a three-year or a one-year licence. This will include confirmation of satisfactory vision. It is useful for carers to keep an eye on the older person's continued ability to drive safely by accompanying them in the car from time to time. Older people and their carers should bear in mind that certain medications can affect driving ability, and any concerns about this should be raised with a GP. People with a diagnosis of dementia may be able to continue to drive for some time, but this should be monitored to ensure that they are safe on the road and not likely to get lost. Signs that older people may no longer be driving safely can include:

- Driving very slowly
- Dents or scrapes on the car
- Difficulty parking
- Confusion about directions
- Driving too close to the edge or drifting into the middle of the road
- Not moving off promptly at green lights

Safe driving requires an ability to react quickly and exercise good judgement, both of which can be affected by dementia or cognitive impairment. Concerns about driving should be taken seriously, as older people are not infrequently involved in road traffic accidents. Family carers should also be aware that even a minor tip can be exceptionally damaging to an older person's confidence.

A geriatrician or GP can refer the older person to a driving assessor who specialises in this area for yearly or six-monthly reviews. The assessor may carry out what is called a Mini Mental State Examination (MMSE) to assess the person's general cognitive condition. The assessors may suggest adaptations to the car, or they may suggest restrictions on driving to preserve safety, such as driving only in daylight, driving within a 5km radius of home, etc. If the person's score for the assessment falls below a safe level, they will no longer be allowed to drive because it isn't considered safe for them to do so. In this case other options can be explored, such as setting up an account with a local taxi company, setting up a family rota of lifts for the older person, buying a motorised scooter, and looking into local bus options. As mentioned in Chapter 5, bear in mind that independence should be preserved where possible, so if the older person has good general mobility, options like taxis and buses may work well.

Adapted car

Where mobility is reduced, a car can sometimes be adapted to accommodate this, and the Disabled Drivers and Disabled Passengers Scheme provides several tax reliefs for drivers and passengers with reduced mobility who use an adapted vehicle. Drivers/passengers may also be eligible for a fuel grant and toll road fee exemption.

Read more

- Citizens Information: tax relief for drivers and passengers with disabilities: http://www.citizensinformation.ie/en/travel_and_recreation/transport_and_disability/tax_relief_for_disabled_drivers_and_disabled_passengers.html
- Revenue Commissioners: importing vehicles: drivers and passengers with disabilities: https://www.revenue.ie/en/importing-vehicles-duty-free-allowances/documents/vrt/vrt7.pdf

---

Mobility parking permit

The Disabled Parking Permit scheme allows approved people to park in accessible parking bays. Holders of a permit can park in these bays free of charge. The permits are available to: 'people living in Ireland with a permanent disability, medical condition, severe mobility difficulties and people who are registered blind, whether drivers or passengers'. The permit can be used in any vehicle in which the holder is travelling, whether as a driver or a passenger. The permit must be displayed clearly on the dashboard of the vehicle in such a way that the serial number, wheelchair symbol and expiry date are clearly visible. Permits must be renewed every two years.

People who are a) Primary Medical Certificate holders or b) registered blind are automatically entitled to a permit on application. An application for a Primary Medical Certificate can be made to the Local Health Office. These certificates are provided to people who are assessed to be severely disabled and permanently disabled for the purposes of the Disabled Drivers and Disabled Passengers Regulations 1994. People in other categories (limited mobility) must make an application with the relevant form to either the Disabled Drivers Association of Ireland or the Irish Wheelchair

Association. The applicant's medical practitioner must complete the relevant section of the form. Under the relevant regulations, a permit is granted to: 'a person with a permanent condition or disability that severely restricts their ability to walk'. This means that people who can walk but who are 'severely restricted' in their walking can apply.

The permit is also known as the European Parking Card and can be used within the EU. They are generally also recognised in the US and Canada. As entitlements under the card vary from country to country, checking the local conditions before travelling is recommended.

Where to get this help

- Contact the Irish Wheelchair Association Parking Section at maats@iwa.ie or tel: 045 893 094/045 893 095. Send applications to: Parking Section National Mobility Centre, Irish Wheelchair Association, Ballinagappa Road, Clane, Co. Kildare. See Irish Wheelchair Association: www.iwa.ie/services/ for full details, *or*
- Contact the Disabled Drivers Association of Ireland, Parking Card Section, at parkingcard@ddai.ie or tel: 094 936 4054/01 6600323. Send applications to: Parking Card Section, Disabled Drivers Association, Ballindine East, Claremorris, Co. Mayo.

Public transport for wheelchair users

Wheelchair users who are in relatively good health should be able to use all types of public transport, including buses, wheelchair-accessible taxis, trains, ferries and planes. Wheelchair-accessible taxis are particularly useful for bringing frail older people to appointments, as the person can sit into their chair at home and be brought from home to the destination without the bother of transferring from wheelchair to car seat and vice versa. Such taxis need to be booked in advance, as taxi companies will have a limited number available.

When driving is no longer possible

It may be very difficult for an older person to hear that they can no longer drive. Many people organise their lives around their cars, and cars give huge freedom in terms of being active and maintaining social contacts. This situation may be particularly challenging for people in rural areas. However, when the older person can no longer drive but remains reasonably mobile, a couple of options are available.

If the older person was previously maintaining a car, the money saved by giving up the car is significant. The average cost of running a car in Ireland in 2017 was estimated at €10,671 (RTÉ, *Motors*, 9 August 2017). The costs include: insurance, motor tax, servicing, fuel, depreciation, NCT costs, etc. Of course, this is an average and many people who use their car lightly will not spend anything like this amount. However, the cost savings of giving up a car are likely to be noticeable for most people. The savings from no longer running a car can be diverted to other forms of transport. Registering with a local taxi company and taking taxis to social events, appointments, etc. is an easy way to replace car-use if finances allow. Using the same taxi company means that the older person will get to know the drivers and vice versa, and it is worth trying to negotiate a monthly or annual rate if the person will use the service sufficiently often. Although it requires an adjustment of attitude, it is a safe and reliable way for older people to remain independent when they can no longer drive. Other options for urban areas include powered wheelchairs and mobility scooters (see the section on reduced mobility later in this chapter). These are becoming more widely used in Ireland, and are very common in the UK and other countries. They provide a good degree of independence for many people with reduced mobility.

Some rural areas have a community-based transport scheme under the Rural Transport Programme (RTP). The programme is delivered by 35 community groups around the country, is open to everyone, and people with a Free Travel Pass may travel free of charge. Where the scheme operates, journeys tend to be local, with the majority delivering people from door to door.

Local Link provides a combination of scheduled public transport services and door-to-door services. There are seventeen Local Link Offices nationwide. These offices manage approximately 1,000 public bus services in local and rural areas of Ireland. Local Link offices open from 9 a.m. to 5 p.m., Monday to Friday.

Where to get this help

- Local Link: https://www.transportforireland.ie/tfi-local-link/
- National Transport Authority, Rural Transport Programme: https://www.nationaltransport.ie/public-transport-services/rural-transport-programme/
- Contact your local Citizens Information Centre for details of any service in your locality.

SECURITY IN THE HOME

Burglar alarms and panic buttons

The installation of a quality burglar alarm can provide a good degree of reassurance about security in the home for an older person. A monitored alarm might be considered if finances allow. Some send an immediate text to family members' mobiles if the alarm is activated. An alarm may be particularly important if the older person lives alone or there are visible signs that an older or incapacitated person lives in the house, such as a wheel-chair ramp or grab rails at the front (if possible these should be disguised by making an architectural feature of them or making them as unobtrusive as possible). In some circumstances, such as where the older person is particularly anxious, lives in an isolated place or has previously experienced a break-in, panic buttons might be considered in the bedroom or in any room with a door to the outside. Pressing the panic button operates either an audible or a silent alarm, and may alert a monitoring centre if the alarm is connected to one. If the older person continues to be anxious, talking to the Community Garda may help.

Deterrents

Following Garda advice on home security, such as 'Lock Up and Light Up', is particularly important for an older person's home. The Gardaí say that most burglars are opportunists and will go for easy targets, so anything that makes entry less attractive is useful. Lights on timers that come on at different times of the day and night are a good idea. Additional locks should be installed if necessary, particularly as many older houses have keyed locks that are easily picked. Doors and downstairs windows should be kept locked when the older person is alone in the house. Sensor lights can be positioned outside the house to detect people approaching at night. A device that detects people approaching the house and activates a sound like a dog barking is also available and may act as a deterrent to unwanted callers. Doorbells with cameras that connect to a display showing who is outside are available and easy to install. Keys should not be stored near doors or hidden under mats. It is often advised that older people simply do not answer the door. If the person calling is a neighbour, friend or family member, they can phone to say they are outside.

Read more

- An Garda Síochána: securing your home: https://www.garda.ie/en/Crime-Prevention/Securing-your-home/
- An Garda Síochána: Lock Up and Light Up campaign: https://www.garda.ie/en/Crime-Prevention/-Lock-Up-Light-Up-campaign/

Where to get this help

- Talk to the Community Garda at your local Garda station.

Seniors alert scheme

Under the Department of Rural and Community Development's Seniors Alert Scheme, which is administered by Pobal, personal alarms are available to older people for security purposes. The alarms consist of a large red button on a bracelet or neck cord. Many older people wear them when at home alone so that in the event of a fall or other mishap, they can press the alarm button to alert the monitoring centre. A grant is available for eligible people to cover the cost of installation of the alarm, the pendant and one year's monitoring, while after the first year the annual monitoring fee is paid by the person directly. Eligibility criteria for the grant include: being aged 65 or over, living alone or with another eligible person, and being of limited means. Family Carers Ireland and other community organisations are authorised to operate the scheme.

Read more

- Seniors Alert Scheme information leaflet: https://sas.pobal.ie/SitePages/Home.aspx

Where to get this help

- Contact a local community group which administers the scheme, Family Carers Ireland or your local Citizens Information Centre.

Providing secure access to the home for multiple carers

When many people need to come and go from the house, it is worth considering mounting a 'key box' on an outside wall. These are like mini safes and can be opened with the right code. The key can be safely stored in the key box, and callers who know the code can let themselves in. This avoids the need to give a door key to everyone, and means that family members who live in the house do not always need to be home to let carers in, or stay up at night until a night carer arrives. Regular changing of the code adds to its security.

PARTICULAR PROBLEMS OR DISABILITIES

Each person will experience ageing differently, with many retaining full, or almost full, use of their faculties and a high level of mobility throughout their old age. However, a majority of people will have difficulty with one or more of their faculties, and may also experience other difficulties such as speaking or swallowing. Many of these issues can be managed and reduced by the use of various aids and equipment. This section discusses some common problems, the professionals who can help and the aids that might assist.

Failing eyesight

Failing eyesight may occur for a variety of reasons. The correct glasses prescription for distance vision (TV and driving), intermediate vision (computer use) and near vision (reading and close work) will help many people. Lenses with distance and reading prescriptions (bifocals or varifocals) are available, eliminating the need for several pairs of glasses. A yearly check-up with an optician will also allow general eye health to be monitored, including assessments for signs of cataracts, glaucoma and macular degeneration. Older people are particularly prone to these conditions, and various treatments are available. A cataract operation may be recommended where necessary, and eye drops may be prescribed if there are signs of glaucoma. Treatment of macular degeneration includes injections of drugs directly into the eye. Dietary supplements may also be recommended. Where the vision cannot be corrected, various aids, such as talking watches and clocks, magnifiers for screens and books, software which reads text on a screen aloud, etc., are available.

Read more

- National Council for the Blind of Ireland: low vision solutions: http://ncbi.ie/our-services

Where to get this help

- Talk to your relative's optician and/or GP.

Failing hearing

Again, hearing loss (presbycusis) is a very common experience as we age. The World Health Organization estimates that about 33 per cent, or one-third of the global population over the age of 65, has 'disabling' hearing loss (this excludes mild hearing loss). Hearing loss can greatly interfere with a person's ability to be independent and to interact and communicate with others. Hearing loss can make it difficult to follow the advice of health professionals, or to hear telephones, alarms or doorbells ringing. Some people experience high-frequency hearing loss, meaning they may have difficulty hearing female voices or high-pitched beeping from an oven. Speech may be muffled, especially in noisy situations. Signs of hearing loss can include:

- Lack of enjoyment of social situations due to an inability to filter speech from background noise
- Having the TV or radio volume very high

- Asking people to repeat what they have said
- Difficulty understanding women's and children's voices
- Difficulty using the phone

According to Chime, the Irish association working for the welfare of deaf and hard of hearing people, individuals wait 'an average of 10 years before seeking help with hearing loss'. Because the onset is gradual, many people take some time to realise they may need help with their hearing, and some may simply not want to do anything about it. However, according to Chime:

> This delay is often unhelpful for the individual. It can make the adjustment and habituation to hearing aids more difficult as the person is older and their brain has become used to a reduced sensation of sound. Chime estimates that in Ireland only one third of people who would benefit from hearing aids have them fitted. Research has shown that people who have acquired a hearing loss but have not been fitted with hearing aids are twice as likely to rely on formal community supports such as meals on wheels or community nurse visits.

On a positive note, the majority of people who have been fitted with hearing aids report that they have a significantly enhanced quality of life and improved communication with family and friends.

If hearing loss is suspected, and if your relative is amenable, talk to the public health nurse or GP. An appointment can be made with an audiologist or other professional to identify the type and degree of hearing loss. They may prescribe a hearing aid, of which there are several types, including behind the ear, in the ear, and mini. There are also assistive listening devices available, which include amplifying devices for phones and hearing loop systems for use in theatres and auditoriums. People on medical cards are entitled to a hearing test and hearing aid free of charge. These can also be accessed privately.

Read more

- Chime: www.chime.ie

Where to get this help

- Talk to your relative's GP about an appointment with a hearing specialist.
- Chime: tel: Freephone 1800 256 257; email: rejoin@chime.ie.

Difficulty eating or swallowing/loss of appetite

A number of difficulties associated with food and nutrition can affect older people, including loss of appetite, difficulty eating and difficulty swallowing. As we age, we engage in less physical activity and so use up fewer calories. Our metabolism also slows down, and as a result we feel less hungry and eat less. To some extent, eating less is a normal part of the ageing experience. Sudden loss of appetite and loss of weight, however, can indicate a health problem and should be investigated by a GP. The advice of a dietician may be useful. Special high-protein drinks may be recommended for certain people; some contain the nutrition of a full meal in the form of a small yogurt-like drink.

If appetite is still present but reduced, carers can encourage the older person to eat by ensuring food is tasty and presented attractively. Small portions mean that the plate doesn't look like a challenge, and an extra portion can then be given if the older person likes. If the person has difficulty eating due to problems with their teeth, make sure the food can be taken in small mouthfuls – chop meat if the older person is not able to do this themselves (remembering the advice on preserving independence whenever possible) and use gravies or sauces to moisten vegetables or potatoes. The older person may prefer two smaller courses to one large one, so portions of fruit (tinned, stewed or fresh) can be offered either as a starter or dessert. Portions of puréed fruit are available from supermarkets. Soups are useful because they are highly nutritious and easy to eat and pulses or wheat germ can be added for extra food value. Yogurts are also easy to eat and nutritious. Processed and sweet foods can be eaten at a sensible level, and the older person should be encouraged to drink as much water as they can. And of course, the day's food and drink intake is likely to involve several cups of tea.

Where to get this help

- Talk to the GP or public health nurse, especially about sudden loss of weight or appetite.
- Get the advice of a dietician, either at your local primary care centre or privately.

Difficulty speaking

A number of health conditions are associated with speech difficulties in older people. Difficulty speaking can be associated with stroke, with a disease such as Parkinson's, or with conditions relating to the muscles involved in speech. Whatever the cause, a speech problem presents particular hurdles for the older person and their carers. It can prevent the older person communicating their needs and wishes, and hinder normal conversation with friends and family. It may cause significant frustration for the older person as they struggle to make themselves understood. Advice should be sought from medical professionals, and if the problem is severe, help should be sought from a speech therapist. Again, the local primary care team may offer the services of a speech therapist, although, like most public health services, there is often a waiting list for appointments. Private speech therapists are available, and some specialise in dealing with older people.

If therapy cannot improve the speech itself, other means of communication may be suggested. Different types of communication aids are available:

- Electronic writing boards or pen and paper can be used if writing is legible, although some frail older people have difficulty writing clearly
- An alphabet chart where the older person can point to letters to spell out words; see Figure 7.1
- A chart specially created for the older person with pictures or symbols showing common things they might want to communicate, for example, 'I'm cold', 'I want to sleep', 'I'd like to walk', 'Please turn on the TV'; see Figure 7.2

Figure 7.1: A simple alphabet chart allows the older person to spell out what they want to say

A	B	C	D	E
F	G	H	I	J
K	L	M	N	O
P	Q	R	S	T
U	V	W	X	Y
Z				

Figure 7.2: A sample chart which an occupational therapist can provide for a person with speech difficulties

I'd like to watch TV 	I'd like an extra blanket 	I'd like a cup of tea 
What time/day/date is it? 	I'd like to listen to music 	I'd like my book please 

Where to get this help

- Talk to the community speech therapist, your relative's GP or the public health nurse.
- Independent Speech-Language Therapists of Ireland: https://isti.ie/adult_therapists/

Reduced mobility

Reduced mobility is a very common problem for older people. Mobility may range from the ability to walk outside unaided or perhaps using a walking stick, to only being able to transfer from bed to chair, to no unaided mobility. Again, several aids and techniques can be used to make the most of an older person's mobility.

Walking outdoors Many older people with some degree of frailty remain able to take short walks alone outside with a walking stick, frame or wheeled walker. Some walkers have a seat and a shopping compartment. These devices can help to maintain independence, especially when the person is content to walk to shops, the church or cafés alone. Family carers may worry about the risk of falls, but a common-sense approach should be taken. As discussed in Chapter 5, the older person may prefer to continue to walk and act independently, tolerating the risk of a fall, rather than become constantly dependent on others. A balance between safety and independence should be sought.

Outdoor mobility with a wheelchair or mobility scooter If walking is no longer feasible, a powered wheelchair or mobility scooter may extend the older person's ability to manage their own shopping and social activities. When purchasing, consideration should be given to the weight of the scooter and how easily it can be put into and taken out of cars.

There are three main categories of battery-powered vehicles available in the market: powered wheelchairs, scooters and buggies. Although still relatively uncommon in Ireland, mobility scooters are popular in many countries and can assist greatly with enhancing quality of life and independence for people with limited mobility. They are available from suppliers of mobility and disability equipment, and can range in size and in price from around €900 to several thousand euro.

Some people with long-term illness cards or medical cards may be entitled to such equipment free of charge if it is recommended by an occupational therapist or physiotherapist. Private health insurance may cover certain equipment. Considerations when choosing a mobility scooter include:

- Where it will be used, i.e. over what distance and what type of terrain
- The user's ability to transfer, i.e. to get on and off the scooter
- The user's ability to steer and manoeuvre
- Whether the user will access buses or trains with the scooter

According to the Road Safety Authority, a mobility scooter is a 'special purpose vehicle', and currently their drivers do not need insurance, tax, a licence or any form of registration. They can be used on footpaths and pedestrian streets, and can enter buildings.

Read more

- NHS (UK), Walking aids, wheelchairs and mobility scooters: https://www.nhs.uk/conditions/social-care-and-support-guide/
- Road Safety Authority, Special purpose vehicles: http://www.rsa.ie
- *Which?* magazine, Choosing a mobility scooter: https://www.which.co.uk/reviews/mobility-scooters/article/how-to-buy-the-best-mobility-scooter/choosing-the-right-mobility-scooter

---

For a funny and interesting take on mobility scooters (and secrets of ageing well in general), see *The Secret Diary of Hendrik Groen, 83¼ Years Old* and *On the Bright Side: The New Secret Diary of Hendrik Groen*, both by Hendrik Groen (aged 85).

Indoor mobility Keeping an older person active within the home is important for preserving independence and also for the value of the exercise it gives. Keep all rooms available to them for as long as possible, including the upstairs rooms. A number of adaptations can be made to the home to aid mobility, including stairlifts, grab rails and ramps.

As previously mentioned, if the older person can use the stairlift without difficulty, do not get into the habit of running up and down the stairs to get things for them: encourage them to be self-caring as far as possible. Walks around the house should be part of the everyday routine; moving around will help with sleeping, eating, digestion and overall health. There are negative aspects to long periods spent in bed or sitting on chairs, including bedsores, stiffness, backache and lowered mood. If care workers call to the house a couple of times a day, ask them to take the older person for a walk during visits. If the older person resists, be gently encouraging. Remember that you are not pestering them – you are doing what health professionals recommend for their own comfort. Of course, use your common sense: there may be days when they have had a bad night and are just too tired, and on these occasions you can let the walk slide. If walks are taken at the same time each day, say mid-morning and mid-afternoon, and become part of the routine, you will not have to negotiate them every day.

As discussed in detail in Chapter 11, grants are available from local authorities for several home adaptations, where eligibility criteria are met, or home adaptations can be arranged privately through many specialist companies.

Finally, make sure that there are no trip hazards where the older person is walking, such as lifting rugs or trailing flexes. Furniture may need to be rearranged to clear central spaces for easier walking, especially if the older person uses a frame. Ensure there is adequate lighting, in particular if the older person has poor vision.

Cognitive impairment

As discussed in Chapter 3, cognitive impairment testing is carried out by health professionals if a degree of cognitive decline or memory loss is noticed. It is important to remember that many older people experience some degree of memory loss, but that this may not affect their ability to function independently. It is only when the cognitive decline affects ability to manage independently that some form of intervention may be needed.

Experts recommend a number of lifestyle habits that can help to minimise the risk of developing dementia and also help people with dementia to live well with the condition:

- Being physically active: at least 30 minutes five days per week
- Not smoking, and drinking only in moderation
- Eating healthily: keeping to a balanced diet with minimal processed food
- Keeping blood pressure at a healthy level
- Keeping the brain active: reading the newspaper, doing puzzles, drawing, painting, doing crosswords
- Taking part in social activities: being in regular contact with people helps to maintain mood and general wellbeing.

One diagnosis that may be made following assessment is what is called mild cognitive impairment. This is a condition involving memory loss, but it does not interfere with independent functioning. Many older people experience short-term memory loss while their long-term memory remains good. Memory aids (see below) can be used to help a person with this diagnosis with daily life. If a finding of impairment is made, medication or other treatment may be recommended, although their usefulness is debated.

Dementia is the other main explanation for memory loss. If you become aware of your relative experiencing significant memory loss or cognitive difficulty, ask the GP or public health nurse for advice. Professional help is needed if a diagnosis of dementia is made, and an appointment should be made with a geriatric specialist. The Alzheimer's Society of Ireland is an excellent source of information and help.

If your relative experiences memory loss, it is wise to consider an Enduring Power of Attorney (EPA), in case the cognitive decline progresses (discussed in detail in Chapter 9). In addition, assistive technology (see Chapter 15) may provide reassurance for both the older person and family carers, especially if the older person lives alone.

Read more

- Alzheimer's Society of Ireland: http://www.alzheimer.ie/Home.aspx
- Dementia information and services: http://dementia.ie/
- Understand Together: http://www.understandtogether.ie/

Memory problems

There are many things you can do to help if your relative experiences memory loss, particularly at the early stages. Simple things such as keeping to a daily routine and not moving household items can help. Other measures include:

- Encourage the older person to write down appointments, including locations, times, the names of the people they are to meet and their telephone numbers. A diary or calendar with this information written down will help both you and the older person.
- Add the contact numbers of family members, the public health nurse and the GP into both home and mobile telephones.

- Set up timers to remind the older person when it is time to take medication. Have a week's supply of the correct medication in a pill box marked with the days of the week and times of the day. In this way all the older person has to do is take the pills for the day/morning/evening when the timer goes off.
- Use sticky notes around the house for short reminders, e.g. how to turn on the hot water or heat.
- Use different coloured caps to distinguish keys, e.g. blue for front door, pink for back door.
- Hang lists of information about regular events, such as the days each bin is put out, on noticeboards.

Another useful strategy is to gather essential information and put charts or lists up in relevant places, for example:

- Leave a list near the front door for the older person to check on leaving the house:

    1. Is the alarm turned on?
    2. Have I got my keys, my wallet, my walking stick and my telephone?
    3. Make sure to pull the door fully closed

- A list in the kitchen of what should be cooked for dinner that day/week
- A list in a prominent place of people your relative deals with regularly, their contact details and what each does, as shown in Table 7.1 below

In summary, tools and aids to memory can include:

- Keeping to a daily routine
- Keeping household items in the same place
- Using a diary or calendar for appointments and social events
- Adding contact numbers for family members, doctors and other essential people into mobile and home phones
- Setting up timers as a medication prompt

- Ensuring that medication for the week is correctly put into a marked pill box at the start of the week
- Making lists or charts of important information and hanging or leaving them in appropriate places, such as by the front door or on the fridge
- Hanging a list of essential contacts where it is easily seen (by the older person and by others in the case of emergency)
- Using sticky notes for short reminders
- Using lists for regular events such as bin days

Table 7.1: A reminder list of people whom your relative deals with regularly

Name	What they do	Telephone number	Where they work
Susan Delaney	Public Health Nurse	01 123 4567	HSE
Mary Murphy	Takes bloods for Warfarin check	01 123 4567	Phlebotomy services
Helen	Care worker, night	01 123 4567	Carers Ltd
Judith	Care worker, day	01 123 4567	Carers Ltd
Lisa	Manager	01 123 4567	Carers Ltd
Liam and Kate	Provide medical help at home	01 123 4567	HSE Community Intervention Team
Ruth	Meals on Wheels manager	01 123 4567	Meals on Wheels
Emma and Paul	Pharmacists	01 123 4567	Pharmacy
Alice	Doctor/GP	01 123 4567	GP's surgery
Stephanie	Receptionist at GP's surgery	01 123 4567	GP's surgery

Read more

- Alzheimer's Society (UK): memory aids, tools and strategies: https://www.alzheimers.org.uk/info/20030/staying_independent/350/memory_aids_tools_and_strategies

Part III

Finances, Managing the Home, and Legal Issues

8

Managing the home and dealing with finances

MANAGING THE HOME

It is time-consuming enough to manage one home without having to manage another as well. In the situation where you are the carer of an older person but do not live with them, you may find yourself managing their home as well as your own. You may need to prioritise, because it is unlikely that you will have the time to attend to everything. In order to establish priorities, a few common-sense issues should be kept in mind in relation to managing your older relative's home:

1. An older person cannot do without heat for any period of time, so make maintenance of the heating system a priority. Arrange an annual boiler service and ensure a continuous supply of oil or

whatever fuel is used. If the house has an open fire or stove, make sure the chimney is swept as needed.

2. An older person may need more light than the average individual, so make sure that replacement bulbs are to hand and change them immediately if they blow. To avoid the risk of falls, ensure there is adequate lighting in every room that the older person uses. Also keep a supply of replacement fuses handy if required.

3. The washing machine is a vital appliance and the contact details of a repair person should be kept handy. Get the machine serviced as required. Some tradespeople will prioritise older people for emergency call outs.

4. Ensure that flooring is safe: inspect for any lifted corners of carpets or rugs that could cause falls. Rugs are a particular hazard. Polished floors may need to be covered with non-slip laminate, as they present a significant fall risk. Heavy-duty tape can be used to tape down corners, but keep an eye out and replace the tape if it frays.

5. If your relative's home is old and lacks insulation, or if the windows are draughty, consider installing ceiling and wall insulation, and replacing windows. Where the older person is confined to the house, the heating is likely to be running almost constantly, and expenditure on insulation and windows may be sensible. The home will certainly be more cosy. Financial assistance for this type of work may be available under the Housing Aid for Older People Scheme (see Chapter 11), and insulation grants and other grants are also available from the Sustainable Energy Authority of Ireland (SEAI) (https://www.seai.ie/grants/).

6. Security is also an important issue for older people, especially if they live alone. Media coverage of burglaries of older people's homes means that security is not just practical but of psychological importance too. Have burglar alarms serviced to ensure all sensors are working. If the older person has a personal pendant alarm (a wearable button alarm linked to a help centre; see Chapter 7 for details), test it regularly to ensure it is working properly. Test smoke alarms and carbon monoxide detectors on a regular basis, and make sure there is a fire extinguisher and fire blanket in the house. It may be helpful to have the fire blanket free or semi-free of its

container so that the older person can access it quickly and use it with ease, without having to extract it from its holder.

7. Keep an eye on everything which requires regular inspection: drains, plumbing, leaks, garden, etc. Although you may not be able to attend to everything, make sure to deal with issues that could cause significant damage if they get worse. Note that Age Action runs a Care and Repair programme whereby they carry out minor repairs in the home for qualifying older and vulnerable people free of charge: see https://www.ageaction.ie/how-we-can-help/care-and-repair   or   phone Dublin: 01-475 6989, Cork: 021-206 7399, Galway 091-527 831.

Checklist 8.1: Checklist of household maintenance tasks

Task	Frequency
Arrange regular boiler service	Annually
Arrange regular chimney sweeping	Annually
Ensure a regular supply of heating fuel	Ongoing
Keep supply of replacement bulbs and fuses in the house	Ongoing
Ensure there is adequate lighting in every room	Ongoing
Arrange washing machine or dishwasher service	As needed
Ensure that flooring is safe; tape down lifting corners if necessary and lay non-slip flooring over polished or slippery floors	Ongoing
Consider insulating the attic and/or walls and replacing draughty windows; grants may be available for this work	Ongoing
Arrange burglar alarm service	As needed
Test personal (pendant) alarm regularly	Monthly
Test smoke and carbon monoxide detectors regularly	Three-monthly
Ensure there is a fire blanket and fire extinguisher in the house	Ongoing
Arrange for car service	Annually or as needed
Book and attend National Car Test (NCT)	As needed

8. If your older relative owns or drives a car, keep in mind that it should be serviced regularly. (Note also the advice in Chapter 7 about keeping an eye on whether your relative is still able to drive safely.)

Where to get this help

- Age Action Care and Repair programme: https://www.ageaction. ie/how-we-can-help/care-and-repair
- Sustainable Energy Authority of Ireland: https://www.seai.ie/grants/

DEALING WITH FINANCES

Establishing trust

Failing to renew house insurance is not uncommon among older people and could be serious if a fire or other event causing extensive damage occurs. In any event, it is a sign that a person is no longer able to manage their own financial affairs. Other signs include letters piling up or bills going unpaid.

This can be a difficult area, as it requires trust between family carer and older person. Even in a family where trust is high, this should be sensitively handled. It is often better to put two carers in charge of managing finances, so that there is less likelihood of any question of poor management or dishonesty arising; two adult siblings or the person's spouse and an adult child might be a good arrangement. If your relative has good cognitive function, they can be consulted on the management of their finances, even if they are happy to leave the actual administration to you. Making a list for the older person of the matters you have attended to can be reassuring and inclusive. It is a respectful way of including the person while removing the burden of the actual tasks. If they are not interested in taking part, whether for reasons of illness or whatever, it is up to you to manage the finances in the best interests of your relative. In most cases this will be straightforward enough – day-to-day management of bills, renewing insurances, paying privately hired carers, etc. Big expenditures, such as buying a new car or getting an extension done, require the agreement of the older person – after all, it is their money. If your relative exhibits progressive cognitive difficulties and there are signs that they may become unable to make their own decisions, an EPA may be needed (see Chapter 9). These are very commonly made, but in many, probably most, cases they are never needed.

Your relative may be very resistant to giving control of, or even information on, their affairs to anyone, even a spouse/partner, daughter or son. Another difficulty is that certain cognitive issues can cause people to wrongly imagine that someone is taking advantage of them or 'robbing them'. If this is problematic in terms of managing finances, talk to your relative's GP or the public health nurse. As with most forms of support that are offered to the older person, it is best to start small. It can be useful to get your relative used to a 'second eye' on their financial and other affairs in small ways, such as the use of letters of authorisation allowing you to pick up parcels/payments/prescriptions or whatever. The concept of the EPA is then less of an emotional upheaval for everyone.

The issue of elder abuse must also be considered. The HSE describes elder abuse as: 'a single or repeated act, or lack of appropriate action, occurring within any relationship where there is an expectation of trust which causes harm or distress to an older person or violates their human and civil rights'.

One form of elder abuse is financial or material abuse; this is: 'Financial or material abuse – including theft, fraud, exploitation, pressure in connection with wills, property, inheritance or financial transactions, or the misuse or misappropriation of property, possessions or benefits.'

Even where there is no question of elder abuse, it may be a niggle at the back of everybody's mind. Always be mindful of the older person's anxieties and involve them as much as possible. If your relative is reluctant to allow you to help with finances, diplomacy will be required, and patience. As mentioned, it may be a case of small steps. A first step might be to set up online banking for your relative, and to carry out transactions online with them present. You will need to provide reassurance that you have their best interests at heart and want to help them rather than take control of their affairs. You might also take part in telephone calls between the older person and insurance companies or financial institutions, with your relative's agreement. If your relative has business or farming interests, or rental properties, you may need to accompany them to meetings with accountants, solicitors or other professionals. Keep your relative involved for as long as possible, as a day will probably arrive when they are relieved to leave the task solely to you.

Practical ways to help the older person manage their finances

The first thing you will need to do is try to get an overview of your relative's finances and business dealings, and to keep this information in a spreadsheet or notebook. It may take a while to put this together if paperwork is scattered, but keep an eye on correspondence coming in, such as bank statements and bills, and you will be able to create a fairly complete picture. It is useful to create a record of finances in the form of a spreadsheet or detailed list of bank accounts, bonds, stocks, etc., as shown in Table 8.1. Gather documents, certificates, bonds, deeds, and any other relevant paperwork, and file them in a safe place. Note that you will need this information if an application is made under the Fair Deal scheme.

As well as knowing what accounts and savings the older person has, you need to also establish:

- What expenses do they have and how are bills paid?
- What income do they have and how is it paid?
- Are they getting all the social protection supports and payments they are entitled to?
- What property do they own?
- What debts or mortgages do they have?

It is also useful to know whether they have made a will and where it is (usually at home in a strongbox or held by their solicitor).

To reduce the work involved in managing finances, automate as much as possible. The two main ways of doing this are:

- Set up direct debits for bill payment.
- Set up online banking for as many accounts as necessary.

It might be a good idea to consolidate bank accounts that have accumulated over the years, again, of course, in consultation with your relative and with their permission. A financial adviser could be approached for advice on the best course of action in the circumstances. Probably, in most cases,

Table 8.1: Spreadsheet or record of bank accounts, bonds, stocks, etc.

Bank and branch/ Company	Name/s on a/c	Type of a/c	IBAN	Balance Dec. 2017	Balance Dec. 2018	Maturity date (if any)	Notes
Bank X, Main St, Drogheda Tel: Email:	Elaine & John Murphy	Savings	XXXX	€4,500.16		N/a	
An Post Tel: Email:	John Murphy	Savings bond	YYYY	€10,000		1 May 2019	
Bank Y, Shop St, Drogheda Tel: Email:	Elaine & John Murphy	Current	ZZZZ	€4,325.10		N/a	State pension and pension from Irish Life paid by electronic fund transfer (EFT) Max. at any time in this a/c should be €5,000
Kerry Group	Elaine & John Murphy						100 Ordinary shares
Eir	E & J Murphy						200 Ordinary shares

tying up savings should be avoided in case the money is needed for medical or nursing care at home, adaptations to the home, or for a nursing home (or even for a holiday if the person is still sufficiently mobile).

At least two accounts should be kept in place:

- A current account for day-to-day finances
- A savings account

It is a good idea to keep a fairly small maximum amount in the current account, in case bank cards are lost or stolen.

In view of the increasing number of frauds, it is also useful to advise your relative that if they receive any calls about their financial affairs they should give no information or personal details and make no commitments; they should notify you and you can respond to the call together if necessary.

Arrange for the state pension and any private pensions to be paid into your relative's account by electronic fund transfer (EFT) to avoid the need to go to the post office – unless of course your relative is mobile and this is something they like to do.

A good way to keep track of the older person's finances is to buy a letter rack and ask them to leave out any business letters for you to look at. Review these once a week with your relative, if possible; deal with anything that needs doing, and file the letters in an expanding file so that you can find them again easily.

If your relative is beginning to find it difficult to deal with companies supplying utilities, phone, broadband, cable TV, etc., it's useful to ring the company with your relative present. Put the phone on speaker and introduce yourself and your relative. Explain that you are helping your relative to manage their account. The staff member can then ask your relative whether they are happy to allow you to talk to them and deal with them about the account. Many companies will make a note on their file that a family member is helping the older person, and retain your name and number on file if the older person gives verbal permission. Note that companies have duties under data protection legislation and are not allowed to give out data except in particular circumstances. Your relative may give consent to their data being shared with you.

Table 8.2 summarises the advice given above in relation to managing your relative's financial affairs. Always consult them and involve them in these activities as far as possible. Depending on the person and their level of frailty, they may be glad to be involved, or they may prefer that you manage things for them.

Table 8.2: Summary of practical ways to help your relative manage their financial affairs

Action

Try to get an overview of your relative's finances and create a spreadsheet or notebook with details, as shown in Table 8.2.

Set up direct debits for bill payment.

Set up online banking for as many accounts as possible.

Consolidate bank accounts if necessary (with permission).

Get financial advice if necessary.

Keep at least two bank accounts:
   A current account for day-to-day expenses, containing a safe maximum amount
   An easily accessible savings account

Arrange for any pensions or other income to be paid into your relative's account by EFT.

Ask your relative to leave business correspondence out in a letter rack for you to look at.

Ring utility and other companies with your relative present and ask them to note on their files your relative's verbal permission for them to talk to you about the account.

Review bank statements and reconcile cheque books with your relative.

Other paperwork

Depending on individual circumstances, there are numerous other types of paperwork that you may need to help your relative with. Some other common tasks are listed in Table 8.3.

Table 8.3: Common ongoing household tasks

Task	Notes
Renew motor tax	Make sure you have the Vehicle Registration Certificate.
Renew car insurance	Note that the insurance company may need to be notified if your relative's health changes, as otherwise the insurance policy may be void.
Ensure that the NCT certificate is up to date	Currently, cars from 4 to 10 years old need to have the NCT carried out every 2 years, while cars over 10 years need an NCT every year.
Renew/review house insurance	Insurance requirements may change if the house is empty for long periods, perhaps while your relative is in hospital. If you employ care workers privately, you may need insurance to cover any injuries they may sustain in the older person's home.
Renew health insurance	If the older person has health insurance, make sure it does not lapse.
Pay monthly utility bills	See 'Dealing with finances' above.

Supplying proof of identity

Banks and other companies have a duty to verify identity under various legislation, and they usually require at least two forms of proof of identity and address, generally a passport or driving licence and recent utility bills. A problem can arise in providing proof of identity for a person in their 80s or 90s if they have not held a driving licence or passport for a number of years. If this is the case, you will need to persuade the company to accept alternative forms of identification, perhaps the older person's birth certificate or their public services card. You may need to speak or write to management to handle this, but bear in mind that they cannot insist on getting documents that do not exist.

Witnesses for documentation

You will sometimes find that the older person's signature on a form needs to be witnessed, and this can cause difficulties if they are housebound or have significant mobility difficulties. For example, most application forms for grants will need to have signatures witnessed, as will certain forms for financial and other institutions. A number of professionals can generally witness signatures, including solicitors and doctors, but these professionals are likely to charge for house calls. If finance is an issue, note that the Community Garda in your relative's local station will call to the house to witness a signature without charge.

VAT refund entitlement

A VAT refund may be given for alterations made to a home to help a person with reduced function carry out daily activities. For more information or to apply contact: Central Repayments Office, Office of the Revenue Commissioners, M: TEK II Building, Armagh Road, Co. Monaghan, H18 YH59; Tel: 01 738 3671.

Read more

- Citizens Information: VAT refunds on aids and appliances used by people with disabilities: http://www.citizensinformation.ie/en/money_and_tax/tax/tax_credits_and_reliefs_for_people_with_disabilities/vat_refunds_on_aids_and_appliances_used_by_people_with_disabilities.html
- Revenue: Form VAT 61A: Claim for Refund of Value Added Tax (VAT) chargeable on aids and appliances for use by Persons with Disabilities under the Value Added Tax (Refund of Tax) (No. 15) Order, 1981: https://www.revenue.ie/en/vat/documents/form-vat61a.pdf

-----

Local Property Tax exemptions

Two Local Property Tax exemptions may be relevant:

Properties vacated by their owners due to illness: this applies where a person leaves their main residence for 12 months or more due to long-term infirmity. The exemption may be available for vacancies of fewer than 12 months where a doctor certifies that the person is unlikely to return to the property, and, in both cases, it applies only if nobody else is living in the house.

Read more

- Revenue guidelines: https://www.revenue.ie/en/property/local-property-tax/exemptions/properties-unoccupied-for-an-extended-period-due-to-illness-of-the-owner.aspx

Property purchased, built or adapted to make it suitable for occupation by a permanently and totally incapacitated individual: in the case of adaptations, the exemption applies only where the adaptation cost is greater than 25 per cent of the market value of the property before it is adapted.

Read more

- Revenue guidelines: https://www.revenue.ie/en/property/documents/lpt/guidelines-reliefs-disabled-incapacitated.pdf

9

Legal issues

ENDURING POWER OF ATTORNEY

If an older person shows increasing signs that they're unable to manage independently, and of memory loss, an Enduring Power of Attorney may be considered. A Power of Attorney is a legal document that allows one person to act for another person. An Enduring Power of Attorney (EPA) is a special form of power of attorney that takes effect only when the person giving the power (the donor) becomes incapacitated. An EPA can be signed by the parties years before it might be needed, as a safety net, and indeed many EPAs are never needed since the donors retain mental capacity until the end. However, if an EPA has been created and the donor becomes significantly unable to manage their own affairs, an application can be made to the Registrar of Wards of Court to register the EPA. If the application is approved, the EPA will be registered and the attorney can begin to exercise the powers given. The High Court has extensive supervisory powers in respect of EPAs. Although creation of an EPA requires the services of a solicitor, it is reasonably simple to arrange and may mean the avoidance of serious problems in the future. If a person becomes mentally incapacitated and does not have an EPA in place, an application to make them a ward of court may be necessary, which is a much more complex process.

Creating an Enduring Power of Attorney

The process of creating an Enduring Power of Attorney has been designed to protect people creating such powers, and a solicitor and a doctor must be involved. The first step is for the older person and, if they wish, a family member, to talk to their solicitor about creating an EPA. During the process, the solicitor will talk to the older person alone to ensure that they understand the nature of the EPA and that they are not being pressured in any way. The powers to be given to the attorney will be discussed and inserted into the document, and a decision made as to who should be appointed attorney. A doctor's statement must be obtained confirming that the donor had the necessary mental capacity at the time the EPA document was executed to understand its effect. The person creating the EPA must also confirm in writing that they understand the effect of creating the power.

Notice of the EPA must be given to two people (neither of whom is the attorney): one must be the donor's spouse/partner if they are living with them. If the donor is not married or is widowed or separated, notice must be given to a child of the donor if applicable, or otherwise to any relative. These are called the 'notice parties'. When an application to register the EPA is made, the notice parties must be notified and can make objections if they wish.

What an EPA contains

The powers given in an EPA can be general or specific. A specific power might be power to sell a house. More likely, an EPA will contain general powers to manage the donor's affairs should they become incapacitated, including managing their property and financial affairs. In addition, an EPA can also contain powers to make 'personal care decisions' for the donor.

Personal care decisions are defined as including the following, although any of them may be excluded:

- Where the donor should live
- With whom the donor should live
- Whom the donor should see and not see
- What training or rehabilitation the donor should receive
- The donor's diet and dress
- Inspection of the donor's personal papers
- Housing, social welfare and other benefits for the donor

It is important to note that personal care decisions do not include health-care decisions.

The donor can appoint anyone they wish to be the attorney (except for the small number of categories prohibited under the legislation, i.e. persons under 18 years, bankrupts, etc.), and may appoint more than one attorney. Often a donor will appoint their spouse/partner and an adult child or two adult children.

Registering an EPA

If the attorney appointed under the EPA believes that the donor has become incapable of managing their own affairs, they can apply to the Registrar of Wards of Court to register the EPA. Before making the application, the attorney must notify the person who made the EPA, the notice parties (see above) and the Registrar of the intention to make the application. Medical evidence that the donor is, or is becoming, mentally incapacitated must be produced. The notice parties can make objections to the application under certain grounds, including that the attorney is unsuitable, or that the donor is not becoming mentally incapacitated. If the application is approved, the Registrar will register the EPA, and the attorney can begin to exercise the powers under it. In simple terms, once the EPA is registered by the Registrar of Wards of Court, the people who have been given powers under the EPA can pay bills from the older person's account and deal with banks and other organisations on their behalf. Note that EPAs are under the supervision of the High Court and an 'interested party' can make an application to the

High Court if they have serious concerns about how the EPA powers are being used.

Read more

- Citizens Information: power of attorney: http://www.citizensinfor mation.ie/en/death/before_a_death/power_of_attorney.html
- Office of Wards of Court: enduring powers of attorney: http://www. courts.ie/

ADVANCE HEALTHCARE DIRECTIVES

An Advance Healthcare Directive (AHD), or 'living will' as it is sometimes called, is a directive about the type of healthcare treatment a person may want in the future should they be unable to make relevant decisions on their care at any time. This is a hugely complicated area, with aspects that extend beyond the personal to consideration of public policy and the public interest. It is also a fraught area, where views can diverge widely. In Ireland, the Assisted Decision-Making (Capacity) Act 2015 contains provisions on AHDs, but these provisions have not yet come into force. It is a grey area under the law currently in operation in Ireland, and the question of whether a particular AHD would be enforceable is open to discussion. Nevertheless, where a person has expressed particular wishes in relation to their treatment, these should be noted and signed in an AHD, and produced when medical treatment is necessary, either at home or on admission to hospital.

The basis of the validity of AHDs lies in the fact that they indicate *lack of consent* to certain medical or surgical treatment. Whether or not a particular AHD would be accepted as enforceable would depend on the exact wording and on the exact circumstances. In Ireland, it is not currently possible for a person who lacks capacity to have someone else make healthcare decisions on their behalf, although they can indicate to their medical team that they would like the wishes of family members or other people taken into consideration. Current medical practice is to consult a patient's next-of-kin if a person is unable to make decisions for themselves.

AHDs are generally used to indicate that certain treatment should not be given. An example of an AHD is a Do Not Resuscitate (DNR) order, which is a statement directing that no extraordinary measures should be taken to prolong life. People also use AHDs to indicate that all possible treatment should be given, but whether this would be enforced depends on the likelihood of the treatment succeeding and on other factors.

Do not resuscitate orders

There may come a point in a person's life when their quality of life is so poor that they make a conscious decision that no extraordinary measures should be taken to prolong their life. If a person is incapable of making such a decision themselves, some families may also reach this decision if their relative has been ill for a long time, has very poor quality of life, and/or has frequently expressed a wish to die. The older person or their next-of-kin can sign a DNR order to be given to medical staff should a critical situation arise. The Irish Hospice Foundation (IHF) has an excellent resource called 'Think Ahead' that offers detailed information on end-of-life planning, and a template Advance Healthcare Directive form is available for download or can be ordered by post. The older person completes the form with instructions for future medical care, and there is also a section for paramedics and medical staff in the event of an emergency (see **Where to get this help** below).

In cases where intervention would only result in prolonging suffering, doctors may ask next-of-kin whether they wish to sign a DNR. It is important to recognise that such an order applies only to *extraordinary* medical measures, which is generally taken to mean cardiopulmonary resuscitation (CPR) in the case of cardiopulmonary failure. All other measures for alleviating the medical situation will be taken as normal.

Currently this is a grey area in Irish law. The Law Reform Commission[28] published a report on the area in 2008, making an interesting observation on the origins of CPR:

> CPR was developed in the 1950s for the purpose of restoring respiratory and cardiac functions to patients suffering a cardiac arrest. CPR was never intended to be administered to terminally ill patients with no hope of recovery.

---

[28] Law Reform Commission (2008) *Consultation Paper on Bioethics: Advance Care Directives*, LRC CP 51.

The British Medical Council has issued detailed guidelines on when a DNR is appropriate (see **Read more** below), including:[29]

- Where attempting CPR will not restart the patient's heart and breathing
- Where the expected benefit is outweighed by the burdens

There were no specific guidelines on DNRs in Ireland at the time of writing, but the Medical Council's *Guide to Professional Conduct and Ethics for Registered Medical Practitioners* contains the following general guidance on end-of-life care:

22.2 There is no obligation on you to start or continue a treatment, or artificial nutrition and hydration, that is futile or disproportionately burdensome, even if such treatment may prolong life. You should carefully consider when to start and when to stop attempts to prolong life, while ensuring that patients receive appropriate pain management and relief from distress.

22.3 You should respect the right of patients to refuse medical treatment or to request the withdrawal of medical treatment. You should also respect a patient's Advance Healthcare Plan.

40.1 Every adult with capacity is entitled to refuse medical treatment. You must respect a patient's decision to refuse treatment.

An advance treatment plan has the same ethical status as a decision by a patient at the actual time of an illness and should be respected on condition that:

the decision was an informed choice, according to the principles of informed consent in paragraph 33,
the decision covers the situation that has arisen, and
the patient has not changed their mind.

---

[29]   British Medical Council, https://www.gmc-uk.org/ethical-guidance/ethical-guidance-for-doctors/treatment-and-care-towards-the-end-of-life/cardiopulmonary-resuscitation-cpr.

41.3 If there is doubt about the existence of an advance treatment plan, the patient's capacity at the time of making the treatment plan or whether it still applies in the present circumstances, you should make treatment decisions based on the patient's best interests. In making such a decision, you should consult with any person with legal authority to make decisions on behalf of the patient and the patient's family if possible.

A tension can sometimes arise between the wishes of the older person and their family, and the inclinations of medical professionals. Medical professionals operate from day to day with the mindset of offering medical intervention to cure illness and alleviate suffering. They may need to adjust this mindset in light of the contrary wish of the older person and their family not to seek intervention in particular situations. If this situation arises, a frank exchange of information and views may be necessary, bearing in mind the guidance of the Medical Council detailed above.

The Irish Hospice Foundation's excellent end-of-life planning resource, the 'Think Ahead' programme, is well worth exploring. The resource contains legal and financial advice, advice on filling the Advance Health-care Directive form, and much more.

Read more

- British Medical Association: Decisions Relating to Cardiopulmonary Resuscitation: a joint statement from the British Medical Association, the Resuscitation Council (UK) and the Royal College of Nursing: https://jme.bmj.com/content/27/5/310
- Department of Justice and Equality, Assisted Decision-Making (Capacity) Act 2015: http://www.justice.ie/en/JELR/Pages/Assisted_Decision-Making_(Capacity)_Act_2015
- General Medical Council (UK): https://www.gmc-uk.org/ethical-guidance/ethical-guidance-for-doctors/treatment-and-care-towards-the-end-of-life
- Irish Health: 'Do Not Resuscitate – who decides?': http://www.irishhealth.com/article.html?id=3475

- Medical Council (Ireland), Guide to Professional Conduct: https://www.medicalcouncil.ie/News-and-Publications/Publications/Information-for-Doctors/Guide-to-Professional-Conduct-and-Ethics-for-Registered-Medical-Practitioners.pdf

Where to get this help

- Irish Hospice Foundation: tel: 01 679 3188, email: info@hospicefoundation.ie: Think Ahead programme: https://hospicefoundation.ie/programmes/public-awareness/think-ahead/
- Irish Hospice Foundation: Emergency Summary form: http://hospicefoundation.ie/wp-content/uploads/2016/07/Emergency_Summary_Form.pdf

FAMILY CARERS IRELAND LEGAL ADVICE SERVICE

Family Carers Ireland offers a legal advice service on issues affecting carers through its partnership with the Community Law & Mediation Centre. Referrals are made through Family Carers Ireland.

Where to get this help

- Legal advice from Family Carers Ireland: https://familycarers.ie/help-and-advice/legal-advice/

Part IV

Help with Care, and Grants and Financial Help

10

Getting help with care

It is worth repeating again and again that caring for a person who cannot be independent for reasons of injury, disability or age is not a solo task. It is very much a team effort. With the best will in the world, no one person can take sole care of a person with extensive care needs. But, on the other hand, a team effort is the best way to care for someone. As discussed previously, a person may respond more willingly to the suggestions of someone outside the family with whom there is no longstanding relationship. This may be in their best interests. A carer will have other people to take over, giving them time to look after themselves, and to maintain their sense of themselves beyond their caring role. The team around the family carers and the older person should include HSE care workers, the public health nurse and staff at the local health centre, the GP, the pharmacist, other family members, and friends of both the carer and older person.

HELP FROM CARERS ORGANISATIONS

Family Carers Ireland Freephone CareLine

Family Carers Ireland (FCI) offers a Freephone CareLine service run by experienced and trained staff. They will listen to any difficulties you want to discuss, and can offer practical advice on carer issues, including the following:

- Carer's Allowance
- Carer's Benefit
- Carer's Support Grant
- Family Carers Ireland services, including respite and training
- Family Carers Ireland carers' groups
- Membership of Family Carers Ireland
- Supports available from your local authority
- The HSE
- The Department of Social Protection

Where to get this help

- Freephone CareLine 1800 24 07 24, lines open Monday to Friday 9.00 a.m.–8.00 p.m.; Saturday 10.00 a.m.–12 p.m.
- Download the FCI information booklets or call the office for a copy:
  » *Rights and Entitlements for Family Carers*: https://familycarers.ie/carer-supports/help-advice/rights-entitlements
  » *The Carers Companion*: https://familycarers.ie/carer-supports/help-advice
- Find your local FCI centre: https://familycarers.ie/help-and-advice/your-local-centre/
- Join the Carers' Coffee Club: https://familycarers.ie/carer-supports/help-advice/carers-coffee-club

Family Carers Ireland Counselling and Advocacy Services

FCI offers 'free, one-to-one counselling to family carers'. A trained counsellor will listen to your concerns and offer help for any issues that the caring role is causing.

FCI also offers a personal advocacy service to help carers deal with health and social services. Often carers will have little experience or knowledge of state services prior to becoming carers. The bureaucracy and paperwork involved in accessing services can be difficult to navigate. FCI can help with 'enquiries, appeals and other appointments with health or social services professionals'. The service has funding limitations, but FCI states that it 'will do [its] utmost to support carers wherever [we] can'.

Where to get this help

- Family Carers Ireland counselling and advocacy service: https://familycarers.ie/help-and-advice/counselling-and-advocacy/ or Careline 1800 24 07 24.

Family Carers Ireland Mentoring and Befriending Services

Family Carers Ireland also offers befriending and mentoring programmes for carers and their older relatives. In the mentoring programme, carers are allocated a former or current carer as a mentor whom they can contact for advice and encouragement.

National Carers Week

National Carers Week takes place in June each year, with the 2020 Carers Week being a virtual event. The week is hugely important for raising awareness of family caring more widely in society through the extensive media coverage that the event attracts. It involves numerous events for family carers. The organisers describe it as 'a celebration and recognition of the role of Ireland's 360,000 Family Carers'. Organisations such as the Irish Cancer Society, the Alzheimer Society of Ireland, MS Ireland and the Irish Hospice Foundation are partners in the week, and organise events for carers around the country. The main objectives of the week are to:

- Raise awareness of family carers in the community
- Deliver events for family carers throughout the country
- Engage with family carers not yet availing of carer support services

Events range from coffee mornings and pampering sessions to seminars, mindfulness workshops and football games.

Read more

- National Carers Week: http://www.carersweek.ie/. To take part email: info@carersweek.ie

---

HOME CARE AGENCIES

The number of home care agencies in Ireland has risen over the past few years from just a few mainly large agencies to numerous agencies of all sizes across the country. Such agencies provide trained care workers on a regular basis. Care can be hired privately or supplied by the HSE as part of a home care package. Quality varies across agencies, as quality of care depends to a large extent on working conditions and training. Workers who have good conditions and who feel a sense of loyalty to their employer are likely to provide a better service, while workers who are underpaid, poorly trained and/or badly treated may find it more difficult to provide good care. The HSE maintains a list of approved providers.

Some care workers work for a short period while they undertake a course of study in a health-related field, while for others caring is a career. Ireland is lucky to have many dedicated and professional carers from outside the country.

One of the advantages of hiring care hours from an agency is that training, insurance and employment matters will be taken care of by the agency, whereas if care workers are hired privately, the person hiring them has the responsibilities of an employer. This is discussed further in the next section.

Hourly rates were approximately €25 at the time of writing. Specialised nursing hours and night hours are more expensive.

Read more

- HSE list of approved home support providers: https://www.hse.ie/eng/home-support-services/approved-home-support-providers/

EMPLOYING CARE WORKERS PRIVATELY

Interviewing

If you decide that private help is necessary, you will need to find and interview care workers. You need to take significant care with this, because the person you hire is likely to spend long periods of time alone with your relative. You need to ensure that at the very least they are competent, experienced, caring and honest. Most care workers will hold a QQI (FETAC) Level 5 qualification in a healthcare-related area, and this should probably be a prerequisite for hiring a private care worker. Garda clearance should also be a prerequisite. Many carers working in Ireland come from other countries, and although perfect English is not necessary, the candidate's standard of English must be sufficient to allow both the older person and you to communicate with them. It is useful for at least two members of the family to meet candidates, as each will have a different perspective. It is also very useful to use a standard list of questions for each candidate; that way it will be easier to compare candidates. Although most people are honest, in such a sensitive situation it is vital also to check:

- **Any references supplied** Make sure to ring the person giving the reference and ask detailed questions. Do not just accept a list of names, or vague assurances over the phone.
- **Any qualifications claimed** Ask to see certificates for each qualification claimed. If they are in another language, typing the text into Google translate should give you a general idea of what the certificate says.
- **Garda vetting** Always ask to see Garda clearance notification. Again, take a practical approach: do not take a stranger's word for it, no matter how honest they appear; ask to see the letter.

Different situations will require different approaches, but you might like to ask some of the following sample questions when interviewing care workers.

Checklist 10.1: Sample questions to ask when interviewing care workers

- What caregiving qualifications/training do you have? Can you provide evidence of these?
- Do you have experience of caring for older people? If so, how old were they?
- What health difficulties did the people you cared for have?
- Do you have training in first aid?
- Have you cared for someone with dementia/reduced mobility/continence issues (or whatever is relevant to your relative) before?
- How far away do you live?
- Do you have reliable transportation? Can you give an assurance that you will always be here on time (barring accidents)?
- Here is a list of caregiving duties. Is there anything on this list that causes a problem or concern for you?
- How would you handle the scenario of my mother waking up at night and wanting to get up and get dressed?
- How would you handle the scenario of my mother appearing to have a fever and lethargy?
- How would you handle the scenario of my mother falling awkwardly and you needing assistance to help her up?

Checking references and qualifications

No matter how suitable the person seems, it is common sense to ask for references, whether written or verbal. Remember that helpers will be in your relative's home, perhaps often alone with them. While most people are reliable and honest, there are of course people who are not. All employers look for references, and people being interviewed for caring roles will expect to be asked for them too. If the interviewee mentions that they have caring qualifications, whether FETAC Level 5 or otherwise, always ask to see documentation. Although you may feel uncomfortable doing this, it is a normal part of the hiring process and interviewees should expect this request. Prepared and honest interviewees should have such documents readily available.

Insurance

You will need to check the insurance situation if you have someone working in your home. Back injuries are very common among carers for older people, and spilled drinks or food can cause falls. If the care worker comes from an agency, they are likely to be covered by the agency's insurance in case of accident, and this should be checked with the agency when making initial enquiries. However, if you are employing someone directly then you may need to alter your home insurance policy to cover this scenario. A serious situation could arise if a care worker is injured in the older person's home and there is no insurance in place.

Legal requirements for employing care workers

If the older person or the family employs care workers directly, someone must register as their employer. The usual employment provisions apply, including payment of PRSI, holiday pay, USC, etc. The Revenue Commissioners' website states:

> If you employ and pay a carer directly, you are their employer and you have certain obligations. You must register as an employer and deduct PAYE, PRSI and USC from the carer's pay.

There are, however, particular difficulties with the employment of private home care workers, and this goes back to the various uncertainties surrounding the caring situation (see Chapter 12). Private home care workers are often employed when crisis strikes – perhaps when the older person's level of dependence jumps dramatically over a short period of time. Families may suddenly find that they simply do not have the hours available or the knowledge to provide all the care required themselves, which may be 24-hour, particularly for a person at end of life. They must then find a suitable carer, interview them, and check references, qualifications and Garda vetting. They must introduce the individual to the older person and try to accustom them to each other. Sometimes the older person, understandably, will not take to a carer, and then the whole process must start again. On the other hand, many private care workers work in the home care field for only a short period of time, perhaps while studying in a health-related field. Ireland is also particularly beholden to migrant carers; as mentioned in Chapter 3, it is probably not an overstatement to say that they form the backbone of the home care service in Ireland. However, people from abroad working in Ireland have their own set of problems, with affordability of accommodation on very modest wages a difficulty, and possibly also visa issues. For these reasons, the possibility that a particular carer will not be around for long is high. In addition, it may be necessary to hire a number of care workers to cover round-the-clock care, and strictly speaking each one should be registered as an employee.

Another uncertainty is changes in the needs of the older person themselves, particularly as they enter the end-of-life stage. Both the older person and their family may realise that they are close to the stage of needing nursing care as opposed to general care. If this would involve a move to a nursing home (if nursing care at home is not financially viable), the tendency for most families will be to hang on for as long as possible. For these reasons, the question of how long the employment will last is relevant to the complexity involved in employing a person. A practical approach is needed, and this is something that should be investigated in conjunction with the new statutory home care scheme.

Read more

- Revenue Commissioners: tax obligations when employing a carer: https://www.revenue.ie/en/personal-tax-credits-reliefs-and-exemptions/health-and-age/employing-a-carer/index.aspx

Introducing care workers to your relative

Depending on their degree of frailty, your relative may see many care workers and professionals throughout the day; perhaps a care worker to help them get up, the public health nurse, a home help to prepare a meal, and another care worker to put them to bed. They can easily get confused when new carers are introduced or when changes are made to their care routine. Therefore it is very important to prepare them when meeting a new care worker for the first time.

Like all relationships, some will work and some won't. You may find that your relative and/or you really likes one or two care workers, while you might be ambivalent about or even dislike others. If either of these things happens, take a practical approach. There is no point in continuing to employ someone who either you or your relative cannot get on with. You can ask the home care agency to schedule specific preferred carers to your relative, or explain that you or your relative would prefer not to have a particular care worker scheduled. Care agencies are used to such requests and will accommodate them where possible. However, due to the shortage of home care staff, agencies often have shortages on particular days and may not always be in a position to comply. When hiring care workers privately, discuss a probation period, long enough to allow the care worker and your relative to get to know each other. If the relationship is not working out, you will have to look again.

Creating a care plan for privately hired care workers

When you employ a care worker privately, you will need to create a care plan containing a list of instructions for the care of your relative, and this will need to be expanded as the older person's needs change. The public health nurse or other health professional can help with this if necessary. Figure 10.1 below gives a sample plan for an overnight care worker.

Figure 10.1: Sample care plan/list of instructions for privately hired overnight care worker

---

Care plan for overnight care workers

Anne is 86 years old and quite frail. She has fallen twice in the last six months and needs support when walking.

HSE care workers come at 8.00pm to help Anne to bed. They come back at 7.30am to help her get up.

Anne occasionally wakes at night, so please respond if she calls. Anne's husband, Paul (83), may get up if he hears Anne. He will help to find anything that's needed.

Please make sure that the following are left beside her bed at night: jug of water and glass, paracetamol, jar with crackers and biscuits, clock.

There is a monitor in Anne's bedroom with the parent unit in the helper's bedroom. She might call if she needs an extra blanket, or help going to the bathroom or taking tablets.

Medication: Anne sometimes has trouble swallowing tablets, so you might need to cut them for her or moisten them on a spoon.

Falls risk: Anne has fallen twice in the last six months so make sure to support her when she is walking.

Diary: Please leave a note in the diary if we need to know of anything that happened during the night, e.g. Anne not feeling well, etc. For anything serious, please contact us by phone. Please ring at any time if you have questions or worries.

Contacts: There is a list of phone numbers on the cupboard in the kitchen. The phone numbers for the out-of-hours doctor and Anne's son and daughter are on the list.

Notes: There is Wi-Fi in the house; the password is xyz 1234. Please feel free to make tea/coffee any time you like, and to use the kitchen. If you need anything, please ask. Thank you.

TRAINING OPPORTUNITIES

Many organisations run training courses for new and experienced family carers. Some of the most common are:

- Manual handling
- First aid
- Dealing with dementia

Where to get this help

- Family Carers Ireland: https://familycarers.ie/help-and-advice/training/
- The Alzheimer Society of Ireland: https://alzheimer.ie/about-dementia/family-carer-training/
- Understand Together dementia training: https://www.understandtogether.ie/training-resources/dementia-training-and-education/
- Acquired Brain Injury Ireland: https://www.abiireland.ie/

11

Grants and financial help

INCOME SUPPORTS FOR CARERS

Family carers may qualify for payments from the state in certain conditions. The number of full-time family carers receiving some form of income support was estimated at 100,00 for 2017 (this includes carers of children with care needs). The main financial supports for family carers of older people are:

- Carer's Allowance
- Half-rate Carer's Allowance
- Care Sharing Payment
- Carer's Benefit
- Carer's Support Grant (formerly the Respite Care Grant)

A brief description of each will be given, but the sources below should be checked for up-to-date information and rates.

Carer's Allowance

This is a means-tested payment for an individual who cares full-time for a person needing full-time care and who will require it for at least 12 months. Certain other conditions must also be fulfilled. See the Citizens Information website at the link below, contact Citizens Information by phone at 0761 07 4000 (Monday to Friday, 9.00 a.m. to 8.00 p.m.), or visit your nearest Citizens Information Centre.

Apply by sending an application form (CR1) to the Department of Employment Affairs and Social Protection (DEASP), Carer's Allowance Section, Social Welfare Services Office, Government Buildings, Ballinalee Road, Longford N39 E4E0.

Forms are available from a social welfare branch office, a Department of Employment Affairs and Social Protection Intreo Centre, or a Citizens Information Centre, or you can download one online at http://www.citizensinformation.ie/en/social_welfare/social_welfare_payments/carers/carers_allowance.html#ld1a9a. The form includes a medical report to be completed by the older person's doctor.

People receiving Carer's Allowance may also qualify for:

- A Free Travel Pass
- The Household Benefits Package
- An increase of 50 per cent in the rate of the Carer's Allowance where more than one person is being cared for
- A GP visit card

Half-Rate Carer's Allowance

The half-rate Carer's Allowance is paid to people who are caring on a full-time basis and who are receiving another social welfare payment (except Jobseeker's Allowance/Benefit and a small number of other payments). People who qualify can keep their main social welfare payment and get the half-rate Carer's Allowance as well. Similar to the full Carer's Allowance, people receiving the half-rate Carer's Allowance may also receive a Free Travel Pass and Household Benefits Package if certain conditions are fulfilled.

Care Sharing Payment

The Care Sharing payment was introduced in 2005 and allows two carers who share care to divide the Carer's Allowance. The care must be provided by each carer for complete weeks, i.e. Monday to Sunday. Carers who qualify will share the Carer's Allowance but each will receive the Household Benefits Package if they meet the qualifying criteria.

Carer's Benefit

The Carer's Leave Act 2001 introduced the right to take unpaid leave for a period of up to two years to provide full-time care for a person in need of 'full-time care and attention' once the carer has worked for the employer for a continuous period of 12 months. The carer's job must be kept open for them to return to after the leave period. Employers can refuse requests for carer's leave only if a period of less than thirteen weeks is requested. Carers who do take such leave may qualify for Carer's Benefit, subject to them fulfilling the conditions and having sufficient PRSI contributions. While on carer's leave, even if you are not receiving Carer's Allowance or Benefit, you are still entitled to social insurance credits. Ask your employer to complete the relevant application form. Further information is available from Citizens Information: http://www.citizensinformation.ie/en/employment/employment_rights_and_conditions/leave_and_holidays/carers_leave_from_employment.html.

Carer's Benefit is paid to people with sufficient social insurance contributions who reduce their working hours to a maximum of 18.5 hours per week with maximum earnings of €332.50 net per week. The person being cared for must be in need of full-time care and the recipient must be a full-time carer. Some other conditions apply.

Apply by completing form CARB1 and forwarding it to the Department of Employment Affairs and Social Protection (DEASP), Carer's Allowance Section, Social Welfare Services Office, Government Buildings, Ballinalee Road, Longford N39 E4E0. The application must be signed and stamped by the applicant's employer and the care recipient's doctor.

Carer's Support Grant (formerly the Respite Care Grant)

The Carer's Support Grant is an annual payment by the Department of Employment Affairs and Social Protection to carers providing full-time care for at least six months a year. Certain conditions apply. At the time of writing the grant was €1,700 per annum. The grant can be spent at the carer's discretion.

More details and up-to-date information on each support are available from:

- Citizens Information Service http://www.citizensinformation.ie/en/reference/checklists/checklist_carers.html
- Family Carers Ireland at https://familycarers.ie/help-and-advice/rights-and-entitlements/
- gov.ie

SCHEMES AND GRANTS FOR HOUSING ADAPTATION

A number of schemes and grants are available to help keep older people's homes in good condition and to adapt them to their needs.

Housing Adaptation Grant for People with a Disability

The Housing Adaptation Grant is available for qualifying people where changes need to be made to a home to make it suitable for a person with a disability. Applicable works include: installation of a stairlift, addition of a toilet or bathroom at ground-floor level, installation of ramps, and changes to create more space. This scheme is administered by the local authorities, and you can get an application form and more information from the local authority housing department.

Applications are prioritised depending on medical need, and an OT's report recommending the alterations is generally needed. The local authority may arrange to get an OT's report, or you can hire an OT privately and reclaim up to €200 of the cost from the local authority. The OT's report should include detailed specifications for the works, which can be given to the builder or installer. Several companies specialise in home adaptations of this type and some have showrooms where you can view stairlifts and adapted bathrooms. You need to supply two detailed quotes for the works with your application. Note that the contractor hired to do the adaptations must provide confirmation of tax clearance to the local authority.

The grant is means-tested, so total household income is assessed. The applicant must also provide details of their tax affairs, which must be up to date, and proof of up-to-date Local Property Tax is also needed. The maximum grant available is €30,000, depending on household income, and the amount reduces as household income increases. Under current rules, no grant is payable where household income is greater than €60,000.

Requirements will vary by local authority, but the documentation commonly needed includes:

- Completed medical report (part of application form)
- Completed tax confirmation form (part of application form)
- OT's report
- Evidence of household income from all sources (usually state pension and perhaps private pension)
- Evidence of age and identity (copy of birth certificate, passport, driving licence)
- Two written itemised quotations from contractors on company headed paper
- Tax clearance certificates for each contractor or registration number and tax clearance certificate number (provided by the contractors)
- Tax clearance certificate for the property owner depending on amount of grant applied for
- Evidence of compliance with Local Property Tax
- In the case of rented dwellings, written permission from the landlord
- Bank account details for payment if grant is approved.[30]

Read more

- Citizens Information: Housing Adaptation Grant for People with a Disability: http://www.citizensinformation.ie/en/housing/housing_grants_and_schemes/housing_adaptation_grant_for_people_with_disability.html

---

[30] Dun Laoghaire Rathdown County Council Form HGD 1.

Where to get this help

- Contact your local authority for full details and the application form.
- Contact your HSE Local Health Office to arrange for an OT's report, or arrange a report privately.
- Contact the Revenue Commissioners to obtain a tax clearance certificate (if required) and confirmation that Local Property Tax (LPT) is paid.
- Contact your local Citizens Information office for help with the form if necessary.
- Ask the older person's GP to complete the medical certificate on the form.
- Get itemised quotes and tax clearance details from two contractors after you receive the OT's report. Your local authority may be able to provide you with a list of contractors that they have dealt with before.

Housing Aid for Older People Scheme

This scheme is intended to improve the condition of older people's homes where they are living in poor housing conditions. The scheme is administered by the local authorities and many of the same conditions apply as apply to the Home Adaptations Grant. The scheme is subject to budgetary constraints, and applications are prioritised on medical and financial need. Highest priority is given where the alterations to the home would facilitate a person being discharged from hospital, or would allow them to continue being cared for at home. The Citizens Information website states that: 'Local authorities have been instructed that only essential repairs should be undertaken to make the property habitable for the applicant.'

Different local authorities have different policies on which types of work they will fund under the scheme, but such works may include:

- Structural repairs or improvements
- Dry-lining
- Repair or replacement of windows and doors

- The provision of water, sanitary services and heating
- Cleaning and painting
- Radon remediation
- Re-wiring
- Any other repair or improvement work considered necessary[31]

An OT's report may be required, and the grant is means-tested. The applicant's tax details must be supplied, and their tax affairs must be in order and Local Property Pax up to date. The contractor hired to carry out the works must also provide confirmation of tax clearance. The maximum grant is currently €8,000. It is possible for an older person to apply for the grant a second time if their needs change significantly over time.

Mobility Aids Grant scheme

The Mobility Aids Grant Scheme is designed to fund works to aid mobility in the home. This can include the installation of stairlifts, ramps, level-access showers and grab rails. This scheme is also administered by local authorities. Note that a refund of VAT paid for aids, appliances and installation may also be available (see Chapter 8). Similar to the two grants described above, priority is based on medical need and highest priority is given to people who are terminally ill, or in situations where the works to the home would facilitate a person being discharged from hospital or remaining in their own home. The grant is means-tested and confirmation that tax affairs are in order and that Local Property Tax is up to date must be submitted with the application.

Read more

- Citizens Information: Mobility Aids Grant Scheme: http://www. citizensinformation.ie/en/housing/housing_grants_and_schemes/ mobility_aids_grant_scheme.html

---

[31] http://www.citizensinformation.ie/en/housing/housing_grants_and_schemes/ housing_aid_for_older_persons_scheme.html

TAX RELIEF FOR CARE PAYMENTS

A person paying for care for 'an incapacitated person' is entitled to tax relief under the Employed person taking care of incapacitated individual relief (there is a separate relief for carers of incapacitated children). The scheme applies to home care costs, nursing home fees and medical expenses. However, uptake of this relief is extremely low – fewer than 2,000 people in the entire country availed of the relief in 2017[32] – which is surprising given that the number of carers for older people is estimated at well over 100,000. The low figure suggests either that people are not aware of the relief, or that in many cases older people are paying for their own care out of savings, and since most older people are not liable for income tax, no tax relief is available. This relief is much vaunted as a benefit to family carers, but in reality it appears to be virtually unused.

THE NURSING HOMES SUPPORT SCHEME (NHSS)/FAIR DEAL

Many people are familiar with the Fair Deal scheme introduced in 2009. Although controversial, it has at least offered some reassurance to older people and their families in relation to the affordability of nursing home care, because there is a cap on the amount that will be charged for care. In addition, the loan part of the scheme (described below) means that repayment is put off until the sale of the applicant's house. Some who work in the area of ageing believe that it compares well to similar schemes in other countries, while others are critical of the scheme.

The process of applying for the scheme is described in some detail below, although the introduction of the proposed statutory home care scheme may supersede the Fair Deal scheme to some extent. However, the application process for the new scheme is likely to be similar to the current scheme, and it is also likely that the nursing home scheme will continue in some form, so the information presented here will continue to be useful.

To summarise the financial aspect of the scheme:

- The older person/applicant contributes 80 per cent of their assessable income to their care and the state pays the balance. However,

---

[32] Care Alliance Ireland (2017) *Trends in Family Caring in Ireland in 2017*, available from: https://www.carealliance.ie/userfiles/file/Overview%20Report.pdf.

in a case where the person's spouse remains at home, they will retain 50 per cent of the couple's income or the maximum rate of the state pension (non-contributory), whichever is the greater.

· The older person/applicant contributes 7.5 per cent of the value of any assets per annum. However, the first €36,000 of the assets (or €72,000 for a couple) is not counted. The older person/applicant's principal residence will be included only for the first three years of care, so that there is a cap of 22.5 per cent of the value of the home no matter how long the person remains in care. If the older person/applicant's spouse remains living in the home, the cap is 11.25 per cent. All other assets are liable to the 7.5 per cent annual charge for each year of care; however, the three-year cap applies in certain situations to farms and businesses.

There are two parts to the scheme:

· **Nursing home support** Payment by the scheme of part of the nursing home costs
· **Nursing home loan** A loan from the state backed by a charge (a type of mortgage) on property

An application can be made for nursing home support only, or for nursing home support and the nursing home loan also.

The application process involves two assessments:

· **Care needs assessment** This involves establishing whether long-term nursing home care is suitable for the older person.
· **Financial assessment** This involves establishing whether the older person qualifies financially for the scheme.

The care needs assessment

The care needs assessment is carried out by a HSE-appointed health professional, often the public health nurse. The assessment can take place in the person's own home or in a hospital or other setting. According to the

Department of Health's explanatory booklet, assessments of the following areas are made:

the older person's ability to carry out the activities of daily living, e.g. bathing, shopping, dressing and moving around,

the medical, health and personal social services being provided to the older person or available to the older person both at the time of the carrying out of the assessment and generally,

the family and community support available to the older person, and the older person's wishes and preferences.[33]

In relation to this last point regarding the older person's wishes and preferences, the relevant part of the assessment reads as follows:

ALL APPLICANTS have the right to self-determination and capacity to do so is assumed unless otherwise proven.

His/her preference to stay at home or to be admitted to residential long-term care must be sought and recorded.

Has the person's above preference been discussed with him/her? Yes No

If YES - brief outline of outcome

If No - Provide a reason and identify with whom it has been discussed & outline outcome.

The information gathered during the assessment is compiled into a document called the Common Summary Assessment Report (CSAR). The report is considered by the HSE, and a decision made as to whether nursing

---

[33]   Department of Health, *Nursing Homes Support Scheme*, version no. 03/17, available from: https://www2.hse.ie/file-library/fair-deal/nursing-homes-support-scheme-information-booklet.pdf.

home care is the most appropriate option. The decision is notified to the older person and their carers by post.

Note that the CSAR is due to be replaced in time with a new standardised tool, the Single Assessment Tool. This will have the advantage of standardising assessments across the country. The new tool involves a much more in-depth assessment of a person's care requirements. As it is technology-based information, details can be stored securely and shared more easily among relevant health professionals. The tool can trigger clinical alerts to prompt the assessor to carry out further medical investigations in certain areas, depending on the data input. The system can also help with care planning. Family carer organisations have welcomed the introduction of the tool but say it is taking too long to be rolled out nationwide. To date, only a pilot project has been carried out.

The financial assessment

The purpose of the financial assessment is to establish what the older person's contribution to the cost of their care will be, and involves disclosure of all the older person's income and assets. According to the definition used in the NHSS information booklet, income includes: 'any earnings, pension income, social welfare benefits/allowances, rental income, income from holding an office or directorship, income from fees, commissions, dividends or interest, or any income which you have deprived yourself of in the 5 years leading up to your application'.

Assets include cash assets such as bank accounts, shares, stocks and securities and non-cash assets such as a house, land or other property. Assets outside the state are included.

For a couple, the assessment will be based on half of the couple's combined income and assets. The assessment takes no account of the income of children or other relatives.

The application process

The first step is to talk to the public health nurse or GP about having a care needs assessment carried out. While this is being arranged, the older person and family can start to gather the information and documents needed for the financial assessment. This involves some work, but it is reasonably straightforward, and it will be useful to have all these documents to hand anyway. Help is available from Family Carers Ireland, the HSE and the Citizens Information Service.

Table 11.1: Some of the main documents required for application for the Fair Deal scheme

Document required	Where to get it
Bank/building society statements	From the financial institutions
Share/bond certificates	In safekeeping at home, or possibly with solicitor or bank
Valuation of property	From a local estate agent
Copy of title deeds to property	Often held for safekeeping by a solicitor or bank; if the property is subject to a mortgage the financial institution will hold the deeds
P60	Pension company or former employer
T21	Revenue Commissioners

The Department of Health's NHSS information booklet contains detailed information on the scheme; call the HSELive team on Callsave 1850 24 1850 or on (041) 685 0300 for a copy of the booklet, or download it here https://www.hse.ie/eng/services/list/4/olderpeople/nhss/information-booklet.pdf.

Read more

- Citizens Information: NHSS: http://www.citizensinformation.ie/en/health/health_services/health_services_for_older_people/nursing_homes_support_scheme_1.html
- HSE, NHSS – A Fair Deal: https://www.hse.ie/eng/services/list/4/olderpeople/nhss/

Part V

Relationships and Emotions

12

The emotional aspect of caring

NATURAL LOVE AND AFFECTION

It goes without saying that the vast majority of caring situations involve love, respect, empathy and a fierce desire to alleviate suffering and offer comfort. Experience of caring varies hugely, and is highly dependent on the level of caring required, the duration of the caring situation, the relationship between the carer and their relative, and the 'burden' on the family carers. This issue of burden depends largely on the other responsibilities in carers' lives. The experience can also vary throughout the caring experience: while in the initial stages the carer may describe their experience in positive terms, as months and perhaps years go by and compassion fatigue or simple exhaustion creep in, the carer may feel much more negatively about their situation. However, looking at averages, many carers report in surveys finding caring 'very rewarding' or 'rewarding'. There are various other reasons why people care for their relatives, and for many the impulse to care is probably based on a combination of reasons including love, duty, a desire to repay, promises made to another parent or relative, and societal expectation.

THE UNCERTAINTIES OF CARING

> In this short Life that only lasts an hour
> How much – how little – is within our power
> Emily Dickinson, *In this short Life that only lasts an hour*

Life is uncertain, but not many life situations have as many uncertainties as a caring role. The impact of these uncertainties make the caring role much more difficult in terms of planning ahead, while at the same time making it essential that family carers do plan ahead. The uncertainties of a caring situation include:

- The older person's level of dependence and the degree of the caring responsibilities
- The duration of the caring responsibilities
- How far finances will stretch
- The carer's other responsibilities – work, children and other dependents – and the changes in these circumstances that might occur with traditional life-cycle developments
- The carer's physical, mental and emotional capacity to deal with their various responsibilities

The process of ageing is a gradual one, and the caring role generally evolves gradually also, intensifying as the older person's needs increase (although in some cases the caring role bursts upon a family after a sudden illness or hospitalisation). As discussed, with increasing dependence comes increasing complexity for family carers, whether in directly providing care, coordinating home care workers, dealing with health professionals, managing medication, accessing supports, managing the older person's home and/or finances, finding suitable aids and appliances, etc. Carers learn as they go along, feeling their way with the help of the primary care team, GP, carers associations and other carers. Uncertainty about the older person's decline often requires that steps are taken to cope with all eventualities, such as putting in place arrangements to manage finances (Chapter 8), creating an Enduring Power of Attorney (Chapter 9), or discussing an Advance Healthcare Directive (Chapter 9).

In an Irish study in 2014[34] the authors stated: 'Respondents [to the survey] indicated that they had been providing care for between one month and 52 years, with the mean time spent on caregiving at seven years.' This huge range in the possible duration of a caring role indicates one of the major uncertainties for carers.

GUILT

Before we discuss anything else, we will meet one of the carer's favourite emotions – guilt. No matter that carers are doing one of the hardest jobs they will ever have to do; no matter that they are putting their lives on hold; no matter that they are performing a Herculean task – carers tell themselves that they're not doing it well enough. They could do more. They could spend more time researching how to do everything better. They could read more literature on how to help their relative emotionally. They could try to spend more time with their children. They could try to achieve more at work. They could try to be sunnier while they're doing everything. Guilt is part of the package.

One of the causes of guilt is the resentment carers may feel at the 'hi-jacking' of their lives and/or at the lack of support from the state and perhaps family and friends. While this resentment may be seen as natural, many carers feel guilty for feeling resentful. Sometimes carers feel that they just do not want to continue doing what they are doing, and this can also cause feelings of guilt.

Some carers, 'sandwich carers' in particular, may experience feelings of guilt because they feel pulled between their various responsibilities and worry that they are not doing anything particularly well.

---

34   Lafferty et al., *Family Carers of Older People: Results of a National Survey of Stress, Conflict and Coping.*

Another possible cause of guilt arises with the onset of compassion fatigue or burnout. Compassion fatigue arises when a person's reserves of compassion become depleted over a long period of time — they begin to experience a feeling that they simply don't care. Burnout is similar to and eventually includes compassion fatigue. It is a condition that creeps up insidiously as competing demands outweigh capacity to meet them. Physical and mental exhaustion are features of burnout, as are anger, resentment and huge guilt.

Some family carers feel guilty at hiring help and not doing everything themselves. This, as we will see, is one of the easiest causes of guilt to let go of, because it is clear that the best care for older people involves a team of family, friends and professionals.

Many carers have times when they feel impatient with or resentful toward their older relative, perhaps at times when the older person's behaviour causes significant difficulty or as a result of the simple frustration that can arise from having to repeatedly explain things or look for lost items. Although this is utterly understandable given the difficult daily conditions, it is a huge source of guilt.

Carers may also feel guilty when conflict arises within the family over the caring situation. This may include feeling angry or resentful toward family members who don't pull their weight or who take major decisions without consulting the other carers.

If a move to residential care has to be considered, for whatever reason, many family carers experience a significant sense of guilt and failure.

With all these reasons for feeling guilty, it is important that carers have strategies to combat what is a corrosive and harmful emotion.

Carers on guilt

Family carer Geraldine Renton on her 'friend' guilt: 'Guilt and I are old friends; guilt never leaves me. I imagine guilt is a friend of every carer on this island of ours.'[35]

Family carer Christina Macdonald on all-consuming guilt: 'I felt guilty when I wasn't with her, even when someone else was taking care of her.

---

[35] https://www.thejournal.ie/readme/column-i-imagine-guilt-is-a-friend-of-every-carer-on-this-island-3435509-Jun2017/

I felt guilty when leaving her after a long visit. I felt guilty if I went on holiday for a few days or went out for a meal with my husband. The guilt was all consuming at times.'[36]

Strategies for dealing with guilt

This quote from a family carer begins to put things in perspective: 'Most carers, it's fair to say, are guilty of one thing: underestimating what a difficult job they do.'[37]

That statement gets to the core of the caring situation for most family carers – carers underestimate the difficulty of the job they are doing. For many carers, it is only when the caring situation ends and the mists begin to clear that they look back in amazement and wonder how they kept going. Keeping this very important insight in mind, we look now at strategies recommended by carers and professionals for dealing with guilt.

Strategies can include:

- Recognising that what you are feeling is guilt; having a name for it is one way to keep it in check. Notice when it arises and carry on. It is likely to always be a part of the caring situation, so teaching yourself to notice it and move on can really help.
- Looking for the main reasons for your guilt; they are likely to be in the list above. When you've found the reasons, think about what changes could alleviate some of these causes. For example, if family conflict is a major cause, perhaps try to improve communication within the family, with help from the public health nurse or other health professionals if necessary, or request or hire more outside help.
- Contacting Family Carers Ireland for advice if you regularly feel impatient with or resentful of your older relative.
- Accepting imperfection: accept that the imperfection arises from the complexity and difficulties of the situation and not from your failings. Remember that nothing and no one could make the

---

[36]   https://alzheimersshow.co.uk/editorial/dealing-carers-guilt/
[37]   https://www.unforgettable.org/blog/dealing-with-carer-guilt/

situation perfect (we discuss this further in Chapter 14). Carers are not magicians.

· Remembering you're not alone: look for carer blogs on guilt and see the similarities with your own situation.
· Reminding yourself occasionally of what a good job you're doing. Imagine what things would be like for your older relative if you weren't caring for them.
· If you feel guilty at not doing everything yourself, remember that the best caring situation involves a combination of family care and help from health professionals and care workers. Lack of a prior relationship and its baggage can be an excellent reason to get help from outside the family.
· Writing down your feelings in a journal or practising mindfulness
· Talking to your GP or asking for a referral to a counsellor

The most important thing to remember is that the guilt is part of the package for every carer, so don't let it overwhelm you.

WORRY AND ANXIETY

Worry is another emotion that goes with the territory of caring: carers worry because there is something to worry about. They worry that their older relative is ill and frail, that they might fall, that they might be in pain, that they might suffer a major health event such as a heart attack or stroke, that finances will not stretch, that they themselves will become ill, that they are neglecting their children/partner/home/work/friends. As such, worry cannot be avoided in a caring situation, so it must be managed. There are a number of techniques that apply generally to the management of anxiety, and some can be readily adapted to a caring situation.

Technique 1 Ignore your worries
Not all worries are real; some worries are caused by physiological factors such as lack of sleep, lack of exercise or poor health. If a worry is of this type, try to ignore it. Like bullies, worries that are ignored often go away, while worries that are given attention often get stronger.

Technique 2 Talk back to your worries

You don't have to accept what your worries are telling you, because it may simply be untrue. As we discuss in Chapter 13, family carers are often exhausted and not at their best during a period of intensive caring, especially during the end-of-life period. The worries therefore may simply be the product of low mood and an inability to think objectively. If this is the case, practice talking back to them. If you experience a general worry that your relative is not getting adequate care, remind yourself that you and the care workers whom you like and trust are providing excellent care, and that in fact the older person is very well cared for. If you worry that something awful will happen, remind yourself that everything has been done to avoid something awful happening (experienced care workers employed, the house made safe, regular contact maintained with the GP), and that if something unexpected does happen, it can be dealt with. If you worry that you are neglecting your children, remind yourself that everyone in the family is affected by the situation, and that it is a normal part of life. Your children are learning to empathise (with the older person and hopefully with you), they may be learning to become helpful, they may also be gaining independence if you are less available to them.

Technique 3 Use the 'worry box' technique

This technique involves creating an imaginary worry box. The box has a strong lock and needs a mental key to open it. To make it more real, you can imagine what the box looks like and what it is made of. The worry box can be opened only at 'worry time'. Worry time is a specific time of day, the same time every day, when you can open the box and see what's inside. At all other times of the day the box must remain locked. When a worry related to the caring situation comes into your head during the day, put the worry in the box. Then, at worry time each day, imagine yourself unlocking the box and looking inside. Do this at a time when you are on your own and nothing else is distracting you. You examine each worry and make a decision as to what to do with it. Some will have evaporated during the day. Some will need action, so you write down there and then what you need to do: make a phone call to get further information, buy an aid which the older person needs, fix something in the older person's house that is a risk, settle some financial matter. The point is that you deal with these worries only *once* in the day, not all day every day, and you tackle them when you are in a position to do something about them.

Remember, though, that anxiety can be a serious problem, and if you are badly affected you should talk to your doctor and/or contact a carers organisation. Healthcare professionals and those who support carers will have seen many carers with anxiety problems before.

ANTICIPATORY GRIEF

All caring is difficult, but as the older person becomes weaker and more ill, emotions come to the fore. Something that many carers of older people do not realise is that they may actually be grieving. It is estimated that about 40 per cent of the general population experience a prolonged period of what can be termed 'progressive dwindling' or 'terminal decline' before death. Progressive dwindling is a term sometimes used by health professionals to describe the tendency over time for people to become more frail and more dependent. This dwindling can last over years, with no outcome possible but death. The MS Unites organisation (an umbrella group of multiple sclerosis organisations) gives this description of progressive dwindling in older people: '[Progressive dwindling] is characterised by chronic accumulation of disability and frailty, and associated with increased dependency and reduced reserves. ... Progressive dwindling is the progressive chronic illness before death.'

Professor Des O'Neill, in his book *Ageing and Caring*, puts the situation this way: '... most causes of frailty in later life are not only chronic, but progressive.'

At some stage during the caring situation for an older person, it may become clear that a tipping point has been reached and that the person is on a decline toward death, although health professionals may or may not expressly state this. However, the situation will probably become clear to the family carers by various indirect means, such as a significant jump in the person's dependency or a change in approach by medical personnel. When this point is reached, carers will begin the grieving process, just as if their relative had actually died. They are grieving for many things at this stage: for the person's pain, suffering and dependence; for the loss of their mother/

father/aunt/uncle as the person they knew; for the difficulty of their task; for their own stress. This type of grief has been called 'anticipatory grief'.

THE OLDER PERSON'S AWARENESS OF DEATH

It is fairly common for older people with low quality of life to express a wish to die. This can be very shocking for family members when they first hear it. They are upset for their relative, who is expressing their level of suffering and distress, and upset at the thought of losing their parent, relative or friend. Knowing that this acceptance of, or even wish for, death is a common feeling in frail older people may be some reassurance. The older person is expressing a level of distress and frustration at what they have lost – independence, mobility, comfort, enjoyment of life. It is understandable and natural that when quality of life becomes very low, some people may view death as a better alternative. Bear in mind, however, that it is important to ensure that the older person is not suffering from a clinical depression that could be redressed by their GP.

This is a difficult issue to handle for family members. How do you react to such a wish? An element of common sense is useful, and obviously any reaction will depend very much on the individuals involved and the relationship. Gentle questioning can help, such as 'Have you been thinking that?' or 'What makes you think that?', and then listening without interruption to the response. A low-key approach is probably best. There is no right way to react, and different members of families will have different reactions. Any response that acknowledges the person's distress is appropriate, such as 'I know it's very difficult ', 'I understand you must be feeling bad'. Religious people might like to be invited to pray about their feelings, or, depending on the type of person your relative is, they might find comfort in a light-hearted response.

Read more

- The Palliative Hub: www.carers.thepalliativehub.com

13

Caring and relationships

An extended family is a network of relationships, and many of these are affected when someone in the family needs care. Carers also find that relationships with friends can be adversely affected by their role. Relationships that can be affected by a caring situation can include:

- The relationship of a couple where one provides care for the other
- The carer's relationship with the person being cared for
- Relationships with children and grandchildren
- Relationships between adult siblings
- Relationships between family carers and their children and partners
- Relationships with friends

THE CARER'S RELATIONSHIP WITH THE PERSON BEING CARED FOR

Most family carers have a good relationship with their older relative. Whether the carer is a person's spouse/partner, child, niece, nephew, other relative or friend, the caring role is often taken on willingly through love and empathy. A major 2014 study[38] found that: 'the vast majority of respondents (87.6%) indicated that they perceived the quality of the current relationship [with the older person] as good or excellent'.

However, although we often think of carers as acting out of love, this is not always the case. Indeed, this issue has been examined recently by Care Alliance Ireland.[39] Carers sometimes resent the assumption that love forms the basis of what they do. Often there is more than one factor involved in the decision to care, of which, of course, the primary one may be love for an elderly parent or other relative. Another factor may be a compassionate human response to suffering. Other factors include the old-fashioned notion of duty; a natural feeling of paying back what parents did for the carer; and societal expectation, or the feeling that society expects adult children to care for their elderly parents in so far as they can. In families with difficult backgrounds, the primary reason may be a sense of duty, particularly where the carer has an ambivalent attitude toward a parent or spouse/partner, or even dislikes them. One difficult situation is where one partner in a marriage that has involved problems of infidelity, abuse or other issues, experiences the onset of disability, and their spouse is called upon to care for them despite the difficult relationship. Adult children may have had difficult relationships with parents, or even experienced neglect or abuse. Although such relationships might be fairly uncommon, they do exist, and it is important that health professionals and support organisations are aware of them and do not take it for granted that every child will want to or be able to care for their ageing relative.

Another aspect of the relationship between family carers and their older relatives is that there is sometimes a lack of appreciation of the effort the carers are putting in, and a lack of thanks for it. For an older person who is

---

[38] Lafferty et al., *Family Carers of Older People: Results of a National Survey of Stress, Conflict and Coping.*

[39] Care Alliance Ireland (2018) *Difficult Relationships and Family Caring*, available from: https://www.carealliance.ie/userfiles/file/CAI_DP8_Difficult_Relationships.pdf.

fully or mostly housebound, time hangs heavy. A day may seem an eternity. They may be unable to appreciate the pressure that their family carers are under, perhaps trying to manage work and childcare as well as their caring role. The reason why you did not ring for three days may be because you have barely drawn breath for three days, but your relative may perceive it as evidence that you don't care enough to ring them, or as a failure on your part in your caring role. This problem is really down to a gap in perception – between your perception of time as a busy worker, parent or both – and the perception of time of an older person with a life that lacks activity and opportunities to socialise. There is no real solution to this, but remembering that this gap in perception may be the reason for a lack of appreciation might help. It is really no one's fault.

Another factor in the possible lack of appreciation of your efforts may be that your relative believes they do not need the care you are giving, or may not even notice it. They might notice that the fridge is empty and there is nothing for dinner, but not that that you are constantly filling it up. They might notice eventually that the laundry basket is overflowing, but may not notice that clean clothes miraculously appear for them each day. They might notice if they have not been out of the house for a week, but not that you arrive regularly three times a week to take them out. In other words, although they would almost certainly notice if you withdrew your caring activities, they may not register that you are providing them. Again, this is really no one's fault. It is something of a product of the ageing experience. At a certain age and state of health, a person's thinking process will change; in other words, the way your relative is thinking may not be the same as the way you and the average adult think. And again, accepting this as a fact of the situation, and as a normal phenomenon, may help you to be less bothered by it.

A final aspect of the relationship between the family carer and their older relative might be that, just as children will reserve their bad behaviour for the place they feel safest – at home with their parents, older people may display their frustration at their frailty and dependence to the people closest to them. Although this is difficult, it is natural. And again, realising that this is a common situation, and that family carers routinely experience this, is a help toward being able to maintain a neutral attitude – essentially to shrug it off.

After the negative aspects discussed in the paragraphs above, we can end with the positives. No matter how difficult the situation is, and how overwhelming you find it, you will always find comfort in the fact that your relative is as comfortable and happy as they could be in the circumstances. Every time you bring them a glass of water, get them an extra cushion, or walk slowly around the garden with them, you are easing their experience of the frailties of old age. And while we discussed lack of appreciation above, many older people will, on the contrary, constantly express their appreciation of what you are doing, or express their regret that you are having to look after them in difficult circumstances. They may tell you that they wish things were otherwise, that they did not need you so much, and that you had more time to do what you enjoy. It is at times like this that you vow to continue until you drop.

THE CARER'S RELATIONSHIP WITH SIBLINGS

There are acres of articles, blogs and advice about the effects of caring on sibling relationships. Unfortunately, these effects are rarely positive. Even in families where sibling relationships have always been good, the strain of an ongoing difficult care situation may lead to conflict.

Sibling relationships in adulthood carry the baggage of childhood and adolescence, and all families have their baggage. Sometimes siblings feel that there is and always has been a favoured child in the family, and this resentment may reappear when caring for a parent, perhaps in the form of the feeling that a parent always notices or praises what one sibling has done for them while failing to notice what others are doing. Siblings may not have been close as children, whether due to differences in age or temperament. As adults thrown together into a caring situation, with all its demands and difficulties, that distance may prove an obstacle to cooperation. Again, siblings may bring the rivalry of their childhood into adulthood, competing with brothers and sisters, even in relation to caring for a parent. Older siblings or those who live abroad may not have seen each other regularly for many years, and are essentially then thrown into a situation that requires huge cooperation and goodwill with people who are almost strangers.

It is vital to remember that *almost all* families will experience relationship difficulties while sharing the care of an older relative, and just knowing this may help ease the tension somewhat. Another important point to bear in mind is that no one is at their best during a caring situation, particularly near the end of life for the older person. As discussed in Chapter 12, adult children of an older person may be grieving as their parent fades away before their eyes and moves toward death. Each will be grieving in their own way, depending on their relationship with that parent, and on their own personal characteristics such as their degree of empathy and their physical and mental resources. Carers are often simply tired and depleted, emotionally and physically. It is no wonder then that conflict and resentment can arise.

Given these factors, if conflict does arise it should not be regarded as yet one more reason to feel guilty. Instead, view it as a natural product of a difficult situation, and resolve to try to keep it in check. A major incentive for keeping relations within the family as good as possible is that it will benefit your older relative, whereas poor relations will probably have a negative effect on them. Another reason is that the caring situation will come to an end, and it would be a shame if family relationships had been destroyed when there are plenty of years ahead to enjoy each other. If sibling carers have children, then keeping good relations with aunts, uncles and cousins is worth pursuing for the children's sake. For everybody's sake it is worth putting effort into maintaining good relationships, and there is lots of advice on how to go about this.

Causes of conflict

In many caring situations where there are a number of adult children involved, there are a few main causes of conflict:

- Division of caring tasks
- Perception of not being kept in the loop
- Perception of one sibling controlling everything/different management styles
- Perception of one sibling being possessive of their parent due to a perceived special relationship
- Lack of appreciation for what others are doing
- Differences of opinion on whether, or what, care is needed

Care Alliance Ireland's recent Discussion Paper *Difficult Relationships and Family Caring* addresses some of these causes:

> Carers describe feelings of frustration due to a lack of understanding from siblings about the actual level of care provided. Communication is key; however, such conversations are difficult to begin and difficult to maintain throughout the entire care journey, which may continue for many years.[40]

Dividing up work

It is probably impossible to divide up caring work fairly, but it is worthwhile making the attempt. The first step, in any event, is to identify clearly what work needs to be done. This can cover areas such as:

- Care within the home during the day, e.g. help with meals, laundry, personal care
- Overnight stays/overnight care
- Managing medication
- Taking the older person to social events or medical appointments
- Shopping for food/clothes/medical supplies or equipment
- Liaising with health professionals and care workers
- Managing the older person's home and/or finances
- Managing paperwork and applying for grants

Once these needs have been identified, an attempt can be made to divide tasks according to each sibling's preferences or availability. One way is to allocate specific days or a set number of hours of care to each sibling, working in conjunction with any paid care workers who are coming in on a regular basis. This may work to some extent, although life tends to inter-vene in the form of work demands, the needs of children, illness or the like. It is worth trying to keep to such a routine as much as possible though, even if just to avoid constantly having to re-make arrangements. Days can be swapped if problems arise.

Another way of dividing up care work is to allocate tasks depending on each person's particular preferences, skills or availability. A sibling with a

---

[40]   Care Alliance Ireland, *Difficult Relationships and Family Caring*.

freer schedule in the mornings might be agreeable to taking their parent to health appointments or daytime social activities. A sibling with no children might be happier to do overnight stays than siblings with young children. Someone with good communication skills might be the best person to deal with health professionals, while someone with research skills might take on the management of finances and other paperwork. Some will find the hands-on aspect of care easier than others.

Ways of dividing up work then might include:

- By time: particular days/hours
- By preference or skill: hands-on care, paperwork, dealing with health professionals and care workers
- By availability: day or night care in accordance with individual circumstances

Things are more difficult when one or more siblings doesn't live in the country, or lives a distance away. In this case the distant sibling may have to fill in on some weekends, or over a week or two during holidays. They might also make a financial contribution toward buying private care. Again, this is a matter for negotiation. As discussed above, a clear requirement before care work is divided up is to establish clearly what is needed. In this discussion, siblings who are with the older person more frequently will generally know better, from simple observation, what is needed. And it must be remembered that functioning can change quickly with older people, so that a couple of months or even weeks can make a significant difference to the older person's needs. Listening to each other and calm negotiation are key to making home care work for elderly parents.

Almost always there is more care needed than siblings feel either willing or able to take on. Again, negotiation will be required, but ultimately someone will need to volunteer to take on tasks they don't want to, or give time they don't have. Until a fit-for-purpose system of state home care emerges, people may need to create time by giving up volunteering roles in sports or other organisations, cutting down on work hours, hiring extra childcare, or whatever. (In the UK, the cumulative effect of carers reducing working hours or leaving the workforce is having a serious effect on the economy, and efforts are being made to tackle this situation, including by the introduction of employment and income support measures [see Chapter 16].) Carers must always keep their own health in mind when making significant life changes, including the decision to cut down work hours or give up work (Chapters 14 and 15).

There are times when siblings either cannot, or will not, take on a share of the care of a parent. There may be a good reason for this, perhaps if the sibling suffers from poor health or has a child with special needs. Sometimes it is simply that they haven't been asked. People may not know how much work someone has taken on, and if they are never asked for help, they may be unaware that there is a problem. Rather than grumble about how so-and-so is doing nothing, it is better to ask them to help, and even to suggest how they might do this. There are cases, however, when such a request will meet with refusal. When there is no obvious good reason for a refusal to take on at least some of the care of an older parent, sibling relationships can suffer serious strain. A refusal to share care puts a burden – often a heavy burden – on the other siblings, and makes life more difficult for them in a very direct way. Again, frank discussion of each sibling's situation in terms of other responsibilities (work, children), health issues (physical/mental health), financial issues, etc. may be needed. Unfortunately some families cannot get past the conflict brought about by this issue when the caring situation ends. Others manage to accept their sibling's decision to refuse to take part, but there may be lingering effects within the family.

Keeping everyone in the loop

Not everyone needs to know every detail, but keeping everyone generally aware of important developments or decisions is vital. When people feel that things are being kept from them, they may decide to step back and to reduce the help they are giving. It is easy and quick to send an email, WhatsApp message or text with important information. It is equally important to assess what is and isn't important, so that people are not swamped with information.

Perception of one sibling controlling everything/different management approaches

Personality will have a big effect on each family carer's way of working. Some people feel more of a need to control things in detail, while others put in the groundwork and then stand back and monitor how things are going. These different management styles in the caring situation probably reflect attitudes to management in life in general. If siblings can appreciate each other's approach, it is easier to deal with this issue, and in fact these different styles can be an advantage in the caring situation. If one sibling tends to manage in detail, that is often very useful. If one wants to do the groundwork and then let the situation manage itself while monitoring it, that approach can suit best in some circumstances. It is important for siblings to manage the situation and not each other, and also to consult one another on important decisions. Again, if a problem arises, open but calm discussion is the best strategy. If siblings can remember that they each have their parent's best interests at heart and are managing as well as they can, then this difference in style becomes less of a problem.

Perception of one sibling being possessive of their parent due to their special relationship

This type of situation may go back to the baggage of childhood, as we discussed above. An older sibling might have helped their mother with the young ones, and may feel a special bond. The youngest sibling might have had a parent to themselves for a time, perhaps after the older ones left home. The person being possessive might not even realise they are acting that way, so simply drawing their attention to it might help. The best approach may be that whatever happened in the past should be left there, and that you are all in it together now and need to get on with things. You might even remind yourselves that you're lucky to have each other to help, because many people are caring alone.

Lack of appreciation for what others are doing

It is impossible for anyone to fully appreciate the ups and downs of someone else's life. It is a part of adult life to experience ongoing difficulties in such areas as work, health, finances, relationships and family life that must be managed, and it is unlikely that anyone will be fully aware of the stresses an individual is under. Because of this, if possible, siblings should try to appreciate what each other is doing, understanding, without being aware of the details, that other siblings are struggling to manage various areas of their lives.

Secondly, siblings are often unaware exactly what caring work others are doing, whether in terms of hours or effort. While time actually spent with the older person is obvious, time spent sourcing an aid or appliance, on paperwork or research, or coordinating health professionals or care workers is not easily quantified and is to some extent invisible. In addition, siblings may experience different levels of effort and strain in carrying out caring tasks, and again this kind of personal experience is unlikely to be obvious.

The best approach here is probably to:

· Listen when a sibling explains what they are doing and what effort it is costing them.
· Remember that the full extent of what a sibling is doing is probably not known to anyone else.
· Offer appreciation for tasks achieved.

Differences of opinion on whether or what care is needed

It is very common for siblings to disagree on the care needed and how best to provide this care. This is partly an expression of the different individuals' personalities and their general outlook on life. It may also occur because of different experiences within the caring situation, or because parents will act differently around different children. For example, one sibling may be present when a parent falls, and thus becomes more concerned about round-the-clock care being needed to avoid a recurrence. A parent may confide more in one sibling than in others and so they may be more in tune with what their parent both needs and wants. Again, a family meeting with an open discussion is the best way of ironing out differences and coming to some level of agreement on the care needed. An outside view from the public health nurse, GP and/or consultant can be helpful in coming to a realistic assessment.

Communicating

The concept of a 'family meeting' may be new to many Irish families. It is a term used to describe an organised meeting between members of a family to discuss a particular topic or agenda. The 'organised' aspect of the meeting is what is important; it distinguishes such a meeting from the normal casual communication that happens within families. To avoid time being wasted, it is useful to decide in advance what topics need to be discussed. This also allows people time to research a particular topic. It might be useful to have family meetings in a pleasant context, maybe a restaurant or coffee shop, so that any tension caused by the meeting might be softened by the pleasant surroundings. Being in a public place will also have a constraining effect on people when expressing their views. It is a good idea to establish some ground rules for family meetings, as they can be tense. The topics under discussion are often difficult or unpleasant, and the baggage of sibling relationships over lifetimes will be brought to the meeting. One important ground rule is that everybody listens to everybody else, and it is wise to have everyone agree to this at the outset. People must be allowed to express their own experiences and be listened to. Research in the area of sibling relationships during a caring situation has shown that simply having concerns listened to and acknowledged by siblings goes some way to keeping relations good. Listening without interruption is key so that each person gets to state their case, express their emotions, describe their concerns, mention their worries, talk about their situation, outline their recommendations and feel that they have been heard. Families as units have different characteristics – some thrive on drama, some hate it. There is little point though in making a grand fuss over small issues in the caring situation, if only because problems will grow as time goes on. If possible, a practical, low-key approach will help.

To summarise the discussion then, a family meeting from time to time can be very helpful in managing the caring situation. For an efficient meeting, one person should be the coordinator and should ensure the following:

- Invite everyone necessary.
- If it would help, hold the meeting over a meal out, but if it might become too tense, then hold it in private in someone's home.
- In advance, ask which topics people would like to discuss and write and circulate a simple agenda.
- If something needs to be researched in advance, ask someone to volunteer to do this and to bring the information along.
- Make sure that at the outset everyone agrees to listen to others without interruption.

- Where the person being cared for is at the end-of-life stage, remind everyone that each one of them may be grieving in their own way. Encourage people to be as careful as possible with each other.
- Make a list of tasks that need to be undertaken and ask for volunteers for each. Each participant should try to ensure that the division of tasks is as fair as possible.
- Try to acknowledge each other's work, particularly if someone has dealt with an exceptionally difficult aspect of the situation or has had a successful outcome with something.
- After the meeting, distribute the list of agreed tasks.

In cases of major difficulty, outside help may be useful. A consultation with a systemic family therapist (www.familytherapyireland.com) may be helpful for some families to facilitate analysis of the situation and to formalise fair plans and rotas that are manageable for everyone.

Activities away from the caring situation

For couples dealing with the demands of work and childcare, the 'night away' is often recommended as a way of reinforcing their bond and giving them a break from the routine. Siblings can benefit from meeting under pleasant circumstances rather than meeting only in the context of the caring situation. It is worth arranging the odd night out for a meal or a drink, or even a night away if this can be managed. Simply spending time together away from the pressure of the caring situation may help to restore relationships that have become tense. It is wise to make a conscious decision to avoid talking about the caring situation during these times, and for everyone to make an effort to keep the tone light.

Communication tools

There are a number of tools that can be used to make communication between family carers easier. Broadcast tools such as WhatsApp make sharing information with a number of people at the same time easier. In this way everyone can be kept in the loop. Like all written modes of communication, you need to be careful of the tone used in messages. As most people know from email, written communication can lack the extra information that talking directly to someone involves, and what is intended as a neutral tone can come across as aggressive or resentful. Be aware of this and keep messages neutral and informative. If something becomes a problem, a phone call might be better, or a longer communication over email.

Jointly is a mobile and online app developed by Carers UK to make caring more organised by allowing easy communication between participants and by collecting notes and information in one place. You create a 'circle of care' for the person you are looking after and invite relevant people, usually the older person's spouse, adult children and perhaps friends. The Carers UK website[41] describes the key features of the tool:

Simple intuitive group communication: Communicate with everyone in your Jointly circle at a touch of a button! Simply post a message or upload an image.

Notes: Keep all your notes together – and never lose them again! Create a health log or store bills using text or image entries.

Tasks/lists: Keep organised and on top of things by using tasks and task lists. Simply create a task and assign it to any member of your Jointly circle, including yourself, and monitor its status.

Calendar: Create date/time specific events and invite anyone in your circle. You can also use the field provided to invite people outside your Jointly circle.

There is also a Profile page to keep useful information on the older person, a Medications feature to keep track of medications, and a Contacts list. The tool is available to download as a mobile app from Apple and Google Play stores.

Read more

- The Jointly app for carers: https://www.jointlyapp.com/#welcome
- WhatsApp: https://www.whatsapp.com/

---

[41]   https://www.carersuk.org/help-and-advice/technology-and-equipment/jointly

THE CARER'S RELATIONSHIP WITH THEIR SPOUSE OR PARTNER

Research has shown that spouses and children of carers are also adversely affected by the caring situation.[42] The caring situation can greatly affect a couple in a marriage or partnership. One partner is experiencing the difficulties, grief and trauma (to whatever degree) of the caring role. The other partner is watching their partner go through this and may feel emotions that range from concern, pity and sorrow to protectiveness and admiration. They may also feel angry at the situation and the lack of support for their partner. Whichever emotions are being experienced by each partner, what is certain is that the partners are being pushed apart by circumstances, in a direct way by the absence of time spent together on their own, and in an indirect way because the carer partner will be absent to some extent from the relationship, or may be emotionally distant, because much of their emotional energy is being used elsewhere.

There are some positives though, and relationships may actually be strengthened by the mutual support partners give to each other throughout the caring situation. Words of support from a spouse/partner can make a huge difference to the carer, and partners might appreciate hearing in return that the carer partner notices and appreciates their support. As a couple, you may be struggling to cope with all your responsibilities, but an indication that your spouse/partner is there for you and admires what you are doing is an invaluable boost. In the same way, support from a spouse/partner at a low point like this will stay with you when your caring role comes to an end. It is not an easy time for anyone, but every kindness now – a shoulder to cry on, help with a task you dread – will outlive the caring role and be remembered.

THE CARER'S RELATIONSHIP WITH THEIR CHILDREN

The stressful effect of the caring situation will extend to the carer's children also. Again, as with a spouse or partner, this will happen in both direct and indirect ways. For children, direct effects will mainly occur due to your absences from home and the time taken up with your caring responsibilities.

---

[42]   Ziemba, R.A. (2002) 'Family Health & Caring For Elderly Parents', *Michigan Family Review*, 7(1): 35–52.

Time spent on caring is time not available for children. You may need to organise school collections or childcare to cover times when you cannot be there. This time factor may also mean that children, for some period at least, may have to cut down on after-school activities, if you or another person is not available to bring them. If this situation arises, don't hesitate to talk to other parents with children in the same club or class; people are, in general, very understanding of the demands of caring and may willingly collect your child and drop them home after the club or class. Many people either have experienced or feel that they will experience the same situation at some stage of their lives, and are happy to help. Another direct effect on children is that less time will be available for your own home management – for cleaning, shopping and cooking. Older children may have to help more at home, and you may have to get used to a house that is not as well kept as you would like. You may have less time to plan, shop for and cook the meals you would like to put on the table, and there might be a period where pizza and ready-meals form the basis of the household's diet.

While children may be delighted to live on pizza, they will notice and be affected if you are sad or stressed, even if you don't discuss the situation directly with them. As we explore in the next section, it is best to talk to your children, as appropriate to their age, about why you are sad or stressed. You can also explain that it is normal that you feel these emotions, that lots of people are in the same situation, and that it is a normal part of life for many families. You can explain what is likely to happen, and involve them in your relative's care – older children may be able to help directly, as described in the next section, and younger children can make drawings and cards to help granny or grandad feel better.

THE OLDER PERSON'S RELATIONSHIP WITH GRANDCHILDREN

It is important to remember that any children of the carer may also be experiencing grief, especially if they have a close relationship with the older person. For the children of carers, the older person is very often a grandparent. Although you may not tell children the exact situation, it is better to be honest with them, as they will probably pick up on the situation anyway from your absences and behaviour. It is also important to prepare children to some extent, especially if your relative has entered the end-of-life stage.

You can start with something simple such as: 'Grandad is very old now and often doesn't feel very well; that's why we look after him.' If they ask whether he will get better, you need to have an answer ready, and parents can make their own decision on this based on the particular characteristics of the child (age, sensitivity, etc.) and the nature of the family relationships. However, at the end-of-life period, it is probably better to make children aware gently by saying something like: 'He might not get better but we'll look after him as well as we can while he's here with us.' This will allow children to begin to accommodate the idea that their grandparent may not get better without the starkness of being told that their grandparent is dying. If your family prays then perhaps get the child to pray for their grandparent in terms of 'Please God look after grandad', rather than praying for him to recover.

Don't keep children away from their grandparents even if they are very ill unless it is absolutely necessary. If a grandparent has experienced a significant decline and looks ill, prepare children for this. Similarly, if there is a lot of medical equipment around the bedroom or house, mention this in advance, but in a casual way. Children will accept whatever adults accept with fortitude and present as natural. If you act naturally around your older relative, your child will do the same. Include them in the care in small ways, fetching blankets or cups of tea, maybe recounting their day, sharing pictures. Don't worry that your relative might find it difficult to hear exactly what is said or to see pictures clearly – the benefit comes from the fact of the interaction rather than the exact nature of it. Older people get great benefit from the presence of children, from their outspokenness, gaiety and spontaneity. Even if the older person does not show much reaction, it is very likely that they greatly appreciate time with their grandchildren.

RELATIONSHIPS OUTSIDE THE FAMILY

Relationships with friends can also suffer as a result of your caring role. Friends may perceive you as distant, distracted, even unreliable. This can happen in particular when your attention is divided – as in the case of sandwich carers – between work, childcare and your caring role. You may find it difficult to socialise, especially if you are experiencing compassion fatigue (see Chapter 16) or anticipatory grief (see Chapter 12) as your relative's life draws to an end, and you may find it easier to withdraw rather than attempt to be sociable when you don't feel like it. There are a few ways to avoid isolating yourself if this is your situation.

- If you are in a club, choir or society, try to keep attending. Some evenings will be okay and some won't, but at least your attention is briefly diverted.
- If you don't feel like meeting friends in a situation where you will have to try to make conversation, try a film, the theatre or an activity like tennis or swimming.
- Try to connect with other carers, especially people who live locally. The huge benefit of this is that you can let your guard down: you won't have to pretend, because you will be with people who understand your situation without explanation, and who can empathise fully. With other carers, black humour (see Chapter 14) may come into play; you can have fun with your situation with others in the same boat, with the resultant release of stress. The importance of other carers cannot be overemphasised, and this is particularly important if you are somewhat confined to the house or if you live in a rural area.

RELATIONSHIP POSITIVES

Having discussed the negative emotional aspects of the caring experience, it is time to look at some of the positives. As we discussed previously, carers may not be at their best during the caring role due to the effects of grief and tiredness. In other ways though, when you are caring you are being the best person you could ever be. Although you may not see it at the time, other people – family, friends and acquaintances – may admire what you are doing, and your strength, resilience and capability.

Friends in need

Many people are lucky enough to have a network of family and friends to help during the caring situation – perhaps friends who you can rely on to pick up children from school if you are stuck, friends who drop in meals or cakes, neighbours who keep an eye on things, people who tell you 'we're there if you need us'. Even if you don't ever need to avail of offers like this, the fact that they are made is reassurance that there is support there. When your caring role ends, you will not quickly forget small kindnesses like these.

New friendships

Another unanticipated positive in terms of relationships during the caring role is the friendships you and your relative may make with care workers. Many care workers have a vocation to care; they may derive huge personal satisfaction from providing care and comfort for an older person. Many come to the role from their own experience of caring for a grandparent or other relative. Some work in the role while undertaking study in health-related areas such as nursing. Generally, home care workers are extremely competent, and many are also warm and empathetic. Of course, there are always some for whom it is a job and nothing more, but even these will be respectful and competent in the main. Often the older person will form a warm relationship with one or two particular care workers, and if this happens you can ask the agency to roster them for your relative as often as possible. You yourself may form good relationships with care workers: after all they may be in your house at all times of the day and night. You may benefit from their companionship as well as from the actual care they provide to your older relative. They will provide reassurance because they will be unfazed by common problems, since they have the training and experience to deal with them, and because they will develop routines with your relative that will allow them to provide the care needed easily and comfortably. You may come to regard them in the light of 'the cavalry' riding to your rescue. Whatever your particular situation, remember that such relationships can happen and can be a positive in the caring situation.

WHEN ONE IN A COUPLE NEEDS CARE AND THE OTHER DOES NOT

The situation when one in a couple needs care and the other does not can complicate how and when caring starts for a family. One partner may be independent, able to get around, able to manage their home and life, and the other may be ill or becoming less independent. Of course, the able partner is likely to be the primary carer, and will probably be able to manage the situation adequately if the care needs are not too high. Problems arise, however, when the care needs increase, or when the primary carer themselves becomes less able to cope. The situation then will involve delicate handling to provide the care needed while allowing the more able partner to retain their sense of control and independence.

Part VI

Coping and Self-Care

14

Getting through and coping

To be able to help another person, you need to be in good health yourself. You need to be physically and mentally well, and you need to maintain your health throughout the period of caring, whether that's weeks, months or years. Research in many countries has repeatedly shown that the carer role can have significant long-term negative effects on carers' health and overall wellbeing. One study[43] summarises how: 'Caring for a "loved one" has long been acknowledged as having real implications for Family Carers' physical and mental health, along with economic, employment and other impacts.' As stated repeatedly throughout this book, it is vital to take care of yourself so that you do not become depleted by the caring role to the point that your own health suffers excessively.

---

[43] Care Alliance Ireland (2015) *Family Caring in Ireland*.

FACTORS INFLUENCING YOUR ABILITY TO COPE

Your ability to cope as a carer will depend on many factors, including:

- The level of dependence of the person you are caring for
- The medical needs of the person you are caring for
- Your relationship with the person you are caring for
- The length of time you have been caring
- Your own physical and mental health
- Your resilience
- Your support network
- Your other responsibilities

In looking at these factors, the first two are self-explanatory: it is common sense that the higher the level of dependence of the older person, the more complex and difficult the task of family carers. Simply dealing with the numerous health professionals involved in the older person's care may be a source of stress, while witnessing your relative's discomfort or unhappiness is likely to cause distress. In addition, day-to-day caring for a person with a high level of dependence will be more time-consuming, and in some circumstances night care may also be needed.

The third factor, the carer's relationship with the older person, is a factor that may be overlooked, but again, it is clear that a good relationship between the carer and the older person will take some of the sting from the caring situation, while a poor or historically difficult relationship will add stress. This is particularly the case where the caring situation continues for a long period.

The last six factors are tightly linked. Resilience can depend on health, other responsibilities and the length of time the carer has been caring; health can depend on the duration of the caring situation, the level of other responsibilities, and the carer's individual resilience to stress.

One of the most common reasons for the end of caring is carer burnout – when the carer becomes physically and mentally exhausted and unable to continue with their caring role. At this stage, the carer's own health is very likely to have been adversely impacted. This is discussed in detail in Chapter 16 in the sections on compassion fatigue and carer burnout.

ACCEPTING IMPERFECTION AND LEARNING TO COMPROMISE

> Forget your perfect offering
> There's a crack in everything
> That's how the light gets in.
>
> Leonard Cohen, 'Anthem', 1992

Accepting that whatever you do it is never going to be perfect is one of the big struggles for family carers. When we start out providing care for older relatives, we often try to make everything perfect. We try to fill in the gaps caused by the older person's dependency, so that life goes on for them as if nothing had changed. We try, in a way, to smooth out the ripples caused by the older person's changing circumstances, attempting to do for them the small number of things that they can no longer do for themselves, and encouraging them to stay as independent as possible. Both the older person and their family carers to some extent try to erase the effects of ageing. However, as the older person becomes more frail and their level of dependence increases, everyone begins to recognise that things have changed for good and that there is no going back. At this stage family carers must begin to change their perception of caring and accept that there is no such thing as perfection in a caring situation, and that no matter what they do, they will never manage the older person's life as well as they could do it themselves. No matter how much attention you pay to their physical comfort, you will not be able to soothe every ache, and no matter how hard you try to provide stimulation and social interaction, you will not be able to remove all of the feelings of distress that come with ageing and dependency.

To preserve your own sanity, you must learn to accept this lack of perfection. A family carer is not a magician, and there is no magic wand that will make everything right. When family carers do their best to look after their older relative, succeeding in some things and failing in others, that is okay. If a walk is missed one day because other things intervene, that is okay. If a hearing aid goes missing for a few days, that is okay. If you spend less time than you would like actually talking to the older person because of all the other things that need to be done, that is okay. As long as the older person is as comfortable as possible, and is provided with as much social opportunity and interaction as possible, you have done your job. There is no point indulging the feeling that someone else would have done it better. Accepting that the imperfection arises from the complexity and difficulties of the situation, and not from any failing on your part, is key to keeping on going, and it is vital to actively try to develop that acceptance.

Read more

• Liddy Manson, 'Let It Be: Accepting Imperfection in Caregiving', https://www.huffingtonpost.com/liddy-manson/aging-parents_b_917219.html

CONSERVING RESOURCES

In Chapter 12 we looked at the uncertainties surrounding the caring role, of which the most problematic is probably the uncertainty surrounding the intensity and duration of the caring situation. Although health professionals may be able to give a general idea, it is simply impossible to predict what level of care will be needed and for how long. This means that family carers must not give everything at the start. However much we might like to do everything ourselves, it is unwise to do so. Every person has a particular physiology with particular physical and mental resources, and we do not know the limits of these until we are tested. Giving everything at the outset from a limited supply may mean ill-health and possibly early burnout. And it is wise, as discussed below, to accept all offers of help.

BALANCING RESPONSIBILITIES

A huge part of maintaining a caring role is quantifying and managing other responsibilities. For many carers, the problem is not the caring role in itself, but the caring role combined with all their other responsibilities. A 2011 study[44] lists 'carer burden' as one of the consequences of competing demands: 'Caregiver burden is related to competing life demands, and the more competing life demands, the greater the opportunity for both

---

[44]   Day J.R. and Anderson, R.A. (2011) 'Compassion Fatigue: An Application of the Concept to Informal Caregivers of Family Members with Dementia'. *Nursing Research and Practice.*

objective and subjective burden.' A worrying and not uncommon effect of overwhelming levels of responsibility is that the stress can translate to frustration and even develop into compassion fatigue or burnout.

With compassion fatigue (also called secondary traumatic stress), the carer reaches a state of numbness, when they feel they no longer care about anything, while burnout may be experienced in the form of physical or mental collapse. When the demand for empathic caring is too much or of too long a duration, or when the balance is wrong and responsibilities are too numerous, the effect may be to overwhelm the carer. One study[45] of compassion fatigue in family carers linked carers having multiple responsibilities to compassion fatigue: 'It is likely that multiple life demands can also contribute to a caregiver developing compassion fatigue.' Multiple life demands for many carers include some or all of the following: part-time or full-time work, caring for young children or teenagers, running a home, providing care for another person, social or civic responsibilities.

How then can a family carer balance these multiple responsibilities? The current answer is that they can't. One or a number of the responsibilities will have to give way to others. This often takes the form of cutting down on work hours, resigning from volunteering roles or giving up the social activities that might have helped them through the caring situation. It also, of course, takes the form of carers neglecting their own health. It is clear that everybody loses in this situation – older people, children and families, carers themselves – and, importantly, society at large. Society loses experienced workers and volunteers when carers have to make these decisions (we discuss the huge effect that the loss of carer workers is having in the UK in Chapter 16), and society loses over the long term when carers' health is compromised and healthcare costs are pushed downstream. The solution is not that carers must manage better, but that society must shoulder more of the responsibilities.

COMPARTMENTALISING

Although it is difficult to do, it is a good idea to get into the habit of putting your caring responsibilities completely out of your mind when your stint is

---

[45] Day and Anderson (2011) 'Compassion Fatigue'.

finished and someone else has taken over. This may sound hard or even callous, but it is a form of self-care. The ability to compartmentalise, or give your attention to where you are and what you are doing in the moment, is a valuable skill.

Once you have done the work of diligently introducing care workers to your relative and helping everyone to adapt to the situation; or of interviewing, vetting and supervising privately hired care workers; and once you and the older person are happy with them and with the care they provide, you need to trust those care workers and give yourself permission to switch off. Although it is a very natural tendency, there is no point in using time away from the caring situation to worry about how things are going. As we discussed in Chapter 10, no one person on their own can take care of an older person – it is very much a team effort. You may be at the centre of the web of support, but you must trust in the ability and empathy of others. As also previously mentioned, your relative may greatly benefit by receiving care from people outside the family who have no long relationship with them to get in the way. Professional care workers are trained in dealing with frail older people, and they have the advantage of distance. Looked at in that way, your absence may be doing your relative good. So, when you take time away from the caring situation, make a conscious effort to leave it all behind, and do whatever else you have or want to do with a clear conscience. If thoughts of problems to do with the caring situation arise during your working day, get into the habit of putting them away until a specific time when you can actually do something about them (see Chapter 12, Worry and anxiety). Teach yourself to compartmentalise and everybody will benefit.

ACCEPTING OFFERS OF HELP

We are very bad as a nation at admitting when something is wrong – everything is always 'grand', even when it's not. The answer to 'How are you? Do you need anything?' need not be 'I'm fine'. As a carer, especially a long-term carer, learn to say 'Yes please, help would be great.'

There are other reasons for accepting help. We have discussed on a number of occasions the uncertainty of the caring situation, in particular the uncertainty around the length of time it will continue for, and the level of care your relative will need. The issue here is that although you may be grand today, if you are still caring in a year's time, will you still be fine? The danger of refusing help is that people may stop offering, thinking perhaps that you are coping fine and unaware that things have become harder. They may think you are insulted or embarrassed by their offer. One way to deal with this is to answer an offer of help with something like 'Thank you. I'm managing fine at the moment, but I might take you up on that offer another time.' This way the person knows you appreciate the offer, but you don't need anything at that particular time, and the offer remains in place to be accepted during tough times.

Remember also that people often like to help. Maybe they would like to help *you* because they're your friend, and to help your relative perhaps for the same reason. They may feel good about helping a neighbour or friend in the same way that people feel positive about volunteering for charities or sports groups. They may be returning a favour for past help they have received from your relative, maybe something that has almost been forgotten and that you may not even be aware of. And finally, they may see themselves in your situation some day, and feel that they will need the help of friends if that day comes.

Learn to accept help from everyone who offers. If a neighbour asks, 'Is there anything I can do?', perhaps suggest they invite your relative for a cup of tea now and then. Opportunities to leave the house and socially interact dwindle greatly when mobility reduces, and a short chat with a well-known neighbour might be the highlight of the day or even week for your relative.

If your relative is generally self-caring but perhaps suffering from dementia and needs to be watched for their safety, it may be possible for neighbours or friends to act as sitters, simply being in the house while you go out for a while. If you have one or two friends or neighbours who can do this regularly for you, you may be able to join a class or gym, meet friends, or whatever. Having a regular outing to look forward to can be very beneficial for your mental wellbeing.

If your relative needs a lot of help at home, you may not be able to leave them with anyone except professional care workers. In that case, maybe a friend could arrange to visit at the same time every week or fortnight. A routine is useful because it avoids the back and forth of setting up visits each time. Carers' social horizons often shrink because of their caring role, and they can sometimes feel divorced from life and the world. They may feel as though they have no 'news', nothing interesting to say, or perhaps they don't always feel like socialising. If this applies to you, maybe you and a like-minded friend could just watch TV or knit or play chess. The organisation Caregiver.org has this advice on asking for and accepting help:

> When people have asked if they can be of help to you, how often have you replied, "Thank you, but I'm fine." Many caregivers don't know how to marshal the goodwill of others and are reluctant to ask for help. You may not wish to "burden" others or admit that you can't handle everything yourself.
>
> Be prepared with a mental list of ways that others could help you. For example, someone could take the person you care for on a 15-minute walk a couple of times a week. Your neighbor could pick up a few things for you at the grocery store. A relative could fill out some insurance papers. When you break down the jobs into very simple tasks, it is easier for people to help. And they do want to help. It is up to you to tell them how.
>
> Help can come from community resources, family, friends, and professionals. Ask them. Don't wait until you are overwhelmed and exhausted or your health fails. Reaching out for help when you need it is a sign of personal strength.

USING BLACK HUMOUR

Black humour or 'gallows' humour is well established as a coping mechanism. People whose job involves dealing with trauma are particularly prone to black humour, including ambulance and fire crews, police, and health professionals. Since caring for a close relative who is sick or dying can be seen as a form of ongoing trauma, it is no wonder that black humour is a coping mechanism for many carers.

Psychologists have studied the reasons why humour helps us cope with trauma and stress. As one author[46] explained: ' … jokes help people cope with the hard times in life. An ability to laugh at rough moments can reduce the negative emotions surrounding a stressful event and also create the positive feelings associated with amusement in general. Put together, those two affective swings can enhance a person's coping powers.'

Another expert[47] explains: 'to the extent you can use humor to change your perspective on things, to see something that is potentially threatening as less threatening, then that allows you to be more efficient in your coping. … just being able to use humor to change the way you interpret a situation – so it doesn't seem quite as threatening – seems very important.'

Comedian Charlie Chaplin put the link between tragedy and comedy this way: 'to truly laugh, you must be able to take your pain and play with it'. Numerous articles and blogs on carers websites confirm the value of black humour. Carer Ruth Huntman shared this on the Carers UK site: 'Dementia is no laughing matter but black humour is my way of coping. So now, instead of looking for the nearest wall to smack my head against I treat most of dad's outbursts as comedy gold for the book or the sitcom I'll never get round to writing.'

She also confirms the enormous value of talking to other carers, people who are in the same boat as you: 'I've felt an instant bond with the other carers I've interviewed. When I'm talking to them I don't feel the need to apologise for feeling frustrated or for my black sense of humour. I've also felt part of a caring family, where situations may be different but we share the same thoughts and feelings.'

It is important to remember that using black humour implies no disrespect to your relative. You are laughing not at them, but at the situation. While you are searching for the fourth time in a day for lost glasses while laundry and cooking and numerous other tasks pile up, you can either laugh or cry. While black humour may shock others, and even shock you at first, you will find it helpful.

---

[46] 'Awfully Funny', *Association for Psychological Science*, 30 April 2013, available from: https://www.psychologicalscience.org/observer/awfully-funny.

[47] Emeritus Professor Arnie Cann of the University of North Carolina, 'Awfully Funny', *Association for Psychological Science*.

15

Self-care

There is an interesting view on the concept of self-care by carers on the website of the Palliative Hub, a resource for the carers and families of those at end of life: 'Many patients feel less of a burden if they see their carers enjoying life and getting a break from their caring role.'

If there is one reason why carers should take care of themselves, then surely this is it. It is not the usual way people view the idea of self-care and the carer, but it is a very useful way of looking at things. In essence, carers can make their older relative feel better by *looking after themselves*, and the corollary of this, of course, is that they can worry their older relative by *not looking after themselves*. A second important reason for carers to look after themselves is to minimise the risk of becoming ill as a result of caring responsibilities. And a third very important reason is that the better their own physical, mental and emotional health, the better they will be able to care for their older relative and the longer they will be able to continue doing so.

MENTAL WELLBEING AND SOCIAL INTERACTION

Surveys by carer organisations reveal that family and friends can fall away when a caring situation arises, particularly when intensive caring is involved. Although they may feel sympathetic, some people cannot cope with the sometimes unpleasant practicalities of the caring situation, and they may stop calling to the house. They may also believe that in keeping their distance they are giving you 'space', because you are so busy with your caring role. Unfortunately, what the carer needs is exactly the opposite – not less social interaction but as much as before, if not more.

It is well established in academic studies that family caring has a negative impact on mental health; this has been shown repeatedly in studies from many countries. We looked in Chapter 12 at some of the reasons for this. Now we look at possible remedies. This is not to say that the stress of caring can be eliminated, but rather that it can be reduced and its effects lessened. One German study from 2016[48] shows clearly how greater social interaction promotes better mental health in carers:

> [Carers] who socialize more frequently enjoy better mental health. We also find that stronger social ties moderate the negative association between caregiving and mental wellbeing. The protective role of social capital appears to be particularly strong for caregivers with high time commitments ...

The UK Department of Health has compiled a list of local authority initiatives aimed at maintaining the mental health of carers. Some examples are:

- Salford City Council and NHS Salford offer a Carer's Personal Budget. Carers can use their personal budget for such things as gym fees, massage sessions, to purchase equipment for hobbies or to pay for trips.
- Derbyshire Council offers personal budgets and breaks including at-home respite and 'sitting services' to allow carers to take regular short breaks.

---

[48]   Thiel, L. (2016) *Caring Alone? Social Capital and the Mental Health of Caregivers*, Berlin: German Institute for Economic Research.

- Lancashire Council's 'Time for Me' scheme offers a grant for things that carers feel will 'give them a break'. One carer bought a sewing machine and started a small business at home.
- Other councils offer carers help to create their own support plans.

Read more

- Lancashire Council: https://www.lancashire.gov.uk/health-and-social-care/adult-social-care/caring-for-someone/

Having things to hold on to outside your caring role

The *Sydney Morning Herald* of 14 June 2008 carried an interview with carers' advocate Sue Pieters-Hawke:

> There was a recent Australian study conducted that showed 'carers as a cohort have the lowest wellbeing and are at high risk of disease and depression'. To combat this 'people who are carers need things that stand outside it; faith, their own identity and activities. You can, for example, lose yourself in young motherhood but hopefully there's the compensatory joy of a baby but if you have been caring for someone in decline then it's very natural and easy to be disheartened by that.'

These 'things to hold on to' can be of any sort: faith, hobbies, work, social events. One study[49] lists the following categories:

- Social gatherings: meeting friends, relatives or neighbours
- Helping: helping out friends, relatives or neighbours
- Political participation: involvement in a citizens' group, political party or local government
- Religious participation: attending church or religious events
- Volunteer work: volunteer work in clubs or social services
- Sports participation: taking part in sports

---

49   Thiel, L. *Caring Alone? Social Capital and the Mental Health of Caregivers.*

- Cultural attendance: going to cultural events
- Entertainment attendance: going to the movies, concerts, dancing or sports events
- Artistic activities: artistic or musical activities

The factors that all these activities have in common include:

- The opportunity for social interaction
- The effect of 'distraction' from the caring role
- The opportunity for a sense of achievement
- The effect of an identity beyond the caring role

Carer support groups and networks

There is nothing so valuable in a difficult situation as talking to people who have had a similar experience. No advice from health professionals (although of great value in its own way) can match the quality of the empathy and understanding that carers get from talking to each other. This is why support groups, whether formal or informal, are a vital part of coping with caring.

As we have discussed, caring can be extremely isolating, particularly for those in rural areas or those whose relative's condition means they are housebound much of the time. All carer organisations, whether local or national, promote support groups. Some organisations have specific, organised meetings for local carers, but if it is difficult to get to such a group, your local carers organisation may be able to put you in touch with other carers in your immediate locality. Family Carers Ireland runs carers groups throughout the country; they meet regularly, generally once a month. Since the Covid-19 pandemic some organisations have set up online carers groups (listed below). According to Family Carers Ireland:

> ... the carers that attend set the agenda. Carers often use the time to share coping strategies and local information in addition to offering emotional support. Guest speakers such as Public Health Nurses, HSE representatives and social welfare experts are invited to meetings to address carers on issues of interest to them. Groups

provide a valuable opportunity to meet others with similar caring experiences. Indeed this is how many enduring friendships began.

Family Carers Ireland lists the benefits of being part of a carers group:

Groups allow carers to:

- Share their experiences, feelings, ideas, concerns, information and problems
- Access information on their rights and entitlements
- Act together to highlight carers issues with decision makers
- Have a sense of connection with other family carers in similar circumstances
- Have a break from the caring situation
- Relax, socialise and learn from other carers
- Cope from day to day

Where to get this help

- Use https://familycarers.ie/find-us/ to get contact details for resource centres that will put you in touch with local groups.
- Care Alliance Ireland online support group: https://www.facebook.com/groups/FamilyCarerOnlineSupportGroupIreland
- The Alzheimer Society online support group: https://alzheimer.ie/about-dementia/family-carer-training/

Learning from other carers: the value of blogs and personal histories

There are numerous personal blogs written by carers detailing their own experience of caring. These blogs can be a good source of information and insight, especially in relation to topics that might be less commonly talked about or unusual circumstances. A word of caution though: the stories in some of the blogs are very sad, and if you are experiencing grief and sadness yourself, it would be better to limit your exposure to them.

EXERCISE, HEALTHY EATING, REST

Almost every article ever written on self-care for carers lists the holy trinity of exercise, healthy eating and rest as essential components of self-care. Of course, these are important aspects of self-care for everybody, carer or not, but they assume particular importance and need particular attention when there is a strong possibility that the carer will neglect them due to busyness, or be unable to find the time for them. For full-time carers especially, a conscious decision is needed to manage these three aspects of self-care, and establishing a routine will help with this. It might be necessary to write a weekly routine with time allocated to exercise and rest. It is easier to keep going with an activity if it is part of a routine, and having such a routine will also allow you to see if circumstances are preventing you from keeping to it. This might also be an indication that your relative's care needs have increased, and if so, this will need to be addressed. A simple weekly routine might look something like this:

Figure 15.1: Sample weekly self-care routine

Monday 2 p.m.	Care worker arrives, walk to village, coffee, walk home
Wednesday 7 p.m.	Care worker arrives, walk with Liz next door
Friday 2 p.m.	Care worker arrives, yoga class in town @ 2.30 p.m.
Sunday 1–5 p.m.	Family member takes over: swim, hike, movie, lunch, etc.

The West Cork Carers Support Group website has some common-sense advice on exercise:

You may feel tired, but regular, moderate exercise will actually give you more rather than less energy. As a bonus you'll sleep better too. You may feel you haven't the time but if you can create just a 20-minute gap in the day, preferably not just before bedtime, it will be worth it.

The secret of effective exercise is to choose an activity that is right for you – one that you enjoy. Simplest of all is a regular, daily walk – round the block, to the nearest park, or to the shops. The closer to home the exercise is, the easier you will find it to do regularly. West Cork Carers Support Group regularly organise courses aimed at improving Carers health and wellbeing. If you can join a class, you will get the benefits of exercise, company and a chance to switch off from your caring role. If you are tense and worried you will also find exercises such as yoga relaxing. If you can't get to a class, you can do these exercises at home with a DVD or book.

If it is difficult to get out of the house, it might be an idea to beg, buy or borrow an exercise machine and put it in the room where you spend most time. If you spend long evenings with your relative in front of the TV, running on a treadmill or cycling mindlessly for 30 minutes while you watch TV will improve your mood and give you a sense of control. Exercise bikes don't take up much room and are relatively cheap to buy; they are often also available second-hand on various websites.

Scheduling routine rest times can be especially important for carers whose older relative wakes often in the night, a situation which can quickly become debilitating and can be dangerous. For example, if you are tired you may have difficulty giving the right medication or you might lose concentration while driving. This should always be discussed with the public health nurse, as the nurse and/or your relative's GP may be able to help with strategies for your relative to sleep better at night, whether by providing greater stimulation during the day, adjusting diet or prescribing sleeping medication. If the situation continues in the long term, then extra daytime care, from whatever source, may be needed to allow you to nap during the day. You are particularly vulnerable to depression and anxiety if you are sleep-deprived, so always treat this seriously.

As regards diet, the usual advice applies: try to eat healthily. If time is a problem, cooking in batches or buying healthy ready-meals might work. Comfort eating can be a problem for carers, and drinking to self-medicate can also be an issue. These are often strategies for coping with stress – but of the unhealthy kind. Be aware that they can arise, and look for advice from other carers, the public health nurse or your own GP if necessary.

REGULAR HEALTH CHECKS

Don't neglect your own health checks: attend your GP, consultant, dentist and optician as necessary. It is useful to tell your doctor about your caring role when you are new to it, as it could affect your physical and mental health, and may help health professionals with diagnosis and treatment. They may also be able to refer you to support services or offer advice. All full-time carers on Carer's Allowance or Benefit are now entitled to a GP visit card.

If your caring role involves lifting, you may benefit from talking to an occupational therapist or physiotherapist, or taking a course that includes manual handling. Back problems are very common among carers of older people.

UNHEALTHY COPING STRATEGIES

As discussed above, carers are human, and some, probably many, turn to unhealthy coping strategies to manage their stress. This may include increased alcohol consumption, comfort eating and drug or tranquilliser use. The extent of alcohol consumption may vary from a glass of something to relax with in the evening to more serious drinking, and most carers will know whether they are drinking for stress relief or as an occasional treat. Comfort eating may occur because a carer is tied to the house and/or bored. Due to reduced opportunities for exercise, overeating may have a serious effect on health. That is not to say that carers should never enjoy a glass of wine or a bar of chocolate, but if any of these habits becomes excessive then there may be a problem, one that could have consequences for both the carer's own health and the quality of care the older person receives. If this is an issue, talk first to the public health nurse or your GP. You can be sure that you won't be telling them anything they haven't heard before. Something about the caring situation may need to change, whether that takes the form of extra cover that allows you to get out of the house more often, a week or two of respite, counselling, or whatever might work best in your particular circumstances.

Where to get this help

- Talk to the public health nurse or your own GP.

NEW SOLUTIONS TO OLD PROBLEMS

A final aspect of self-care is allowing technology to do some of the work. As the global population ages and doubts continue about the availability of the workforce that will be needed to undertake the care of frail older people, new technologies are being developed to assist with that work. Most of us now use technology on a daily basis, so the use of technology in the caring area is a natural development that could have wide-ranging benefits for older people and carers alike. The Carers UK report *Potential for Change*[50] sees opportunities for the health system, carers and families, employers and the economy in the adoption of technology in the area of healthcare and caring. Some of the emerging solutions are briefly described here, and some of the products described are currently available in Ireland.

Ambient assisted living technology

Ambient assisted living (AAL) technology has been described as: 'concepts, products and services which combine new technologies and the social environment in order to improve quality of life in all periods of life'.[51] A European-wide AAL programme funds projects that work toward creating products and services for older people. The projects address issues such as 'management of chronic conditions, social inclusion, access to online services, mobility, management of daily activities, and support from informal carers'. Products that fall within the description range from wearable sensors to networked kitchen/shop environments to smartphone 'virtual companions' which can prevent older people getting lost.

---

[50] Carers UK (2013) *Potential for Change: Transforming Public Awareness and Demand for Health and Care Technology*, available from https://www.carersuk.org/files/section/4827/uk4062-potential-for-change.pdf.

[51] Xenakidis, C.N., Hadjiantonis, A.M. and Milis, G.M. (2015) 'Assistive Technologies for People with Dementia' in P.D. Bamidis (ed), *Handbook of Research on Innovations in the Diagnosis and Treatment of Dementia*, Harrisburg, PA: Idea Group, 268–289.

Telecare

Telecare is technology used to aid the provision of care. Carers UK[52] describes Telecare as 'a system of monitors and sensors which can include a basic alarm service, able to respond 24/7, e.g. if someone has a fall. It can include sensors such as motion or fall detectors and fire and gas alarms that trigger an alert to a response centre staffed 24 hours a day, 365 days a year. It can include location devices that can find someone, e.g. if someone with dementia wanders outside the home.'

Sensors can alert the carer if a window or door has been opened, or if someone is moving around a room or gets out of bed. This sort of system can enable carers and the older person to be in different rooms or different parts of the house, each getting on with their own activities. The older person can have a degree of privacy and independence and the carer has the reassurance that they will be alerted when necessary.

CCTV

Some families find CCTV useful, although it should be considered carefully before installation. It may allow the older person more independence, and allay the carer's anxiety, especially if the older person is particularly frail or at risk of falls or other medical events. It can allow the carer to monitor whether the older person is safe while they are away from the house. Within the home, carer and older person can be in different parts of the house while the carer keeps an eye on their relative via the monitor. Cameras can be placed in certain rooms only, allowing maximum privacy to the older person.

Telehealth

Telehealth is essentially the use of technology for providing health services and distributing health information. It enables communication between the patient and the doctor without the necessity for them to be in the same place, and allows advice, reminders and education to be delivered by the use of technology. An aspect of Telehealth is Remote Patient Monitoring (RPM), which is the use of a system of sensors and monitors that gathers information about aspects of a person's health and transmits it to their health professionals. In this way, problems can be identified early and

---

[52]   Carers UK, *Potential for Change*.

acted upon. Computers, sensors and wearable devices gather and transmit data on the person's health, such as blood pressure and glucose concentration values. Telehealth systems are currently being developed in Ireland and other countries. Remote patient monitoring devices can also be used to detect falls by the use of sensors. Telehealth hubs are in operation in the UK, with one such being the Airedale Telehealth Hub.[53] The hub 'provides remote support to patients and carers via a video link, with the aim of reducing attendances to A&E and admissions into the hospital. The service provides … advice to patients, and coordinates referral to other services where required.' Patients and carers can make a video call to health professionals on a 24-hour basis, which often provides them with reassurance and avoids unnecessary hospital attendances. The scheme has been shown to have significantly reduced A&E attendance and hospital admissions.

Read more

- A place for mom blog: Ambient Assisted Living: https://www.aplaceformom.com/blog/10-29-14-ambient-assisted-living/
- Ambient Assisted Living Programme: ageing well in the digital world: http://www.aal-europe.eu/
- Telehealth Hub: Airedale NHS Foundation Trust: https://assets.publishing.service.gov.uk/government/uploads/system/uploads/attachment_data/file/458974/Airedale_.pdf

---

53   Telehealth Hub: Airedale NHS Foundation Trust: https://assets.publishing.service.gov.uk/government/uploads/system/uploads/attachment_data/file/458974/Airedale_.pdf

Part VII

Challenges for Carers and Society

16

The negative effects of caring and some ways to combat them

We look in this chapter at the negative effects that caring can have on family carers, in particular at the issues of compassion fatigue and carer burnout. The chapter then examines how other countries assess carers' needs, and carer supports that may go some way toward combatting the negative effects discussed.

Caring for an older person at home comes to an end for many families when it becomes necessary for the older person to move to a nursing home. The two main reasons why older people move to nursing home care are: 1) they become so frail and ill that they need medical care that cannot be provided at home, or 2) their family carers can no longer provide care at home because it is too difficult or too expensive or both.

As discussed in earlier chapters, It has been established beyond doubt in numerous academic studies that caring can negatively affect carer wellbeing. A 2016 German study of the mental health of caregivers[54] clearly stated the link between family caring and mental wellbeing: 'research suggests that caregivers more frequently report greater degrees of depression, anxiety, or stress and exhibit lower levels of subjective wellbeing than non-caregivers.'

COMPASSION FATIGUE

> Too long a sacrifice
> Can make a stone of the heart.
>
> WB Yeats, *Easter, 1916*

It has long been recognised that compassion can fade over time. Most of us will be familiar with the term 'sympathy fatigue' or 'compassion fatigue', often used in relation to healthcare professionals who experience reduced capacity to help after being exposed over a long period to the distress of their patients, or in relation to the difficulties that charities face in continuously fundraising. Human beings, it seems, have a pool of compassion that can be drained over time.

The concept of 'compassion fatigue' developed in the 1980s, with Charles Figley, one of the originators of the concept, describing it as: 'the cost of caring for others [who are] in emotional pain'. One formal description of compassion fatigue describes it as: 'the overall experience of emotional and physical fatigue that social service professionals experience due to chronic use of empathy when engaging with service users who are suffering in some way'.[55] It is no surprise that carers are susceptible to compassion fatigue. Carers, like social service professionals, are

---

54   L Thiel, *Caring Alone? Social Capital and the Mental Health of Caregivers.*

55   Newell, J.M and MacNeil, G.A. (2010) 'Professional Burnout, Vicarious Trauma, Secondary Traumatic Stress, and Compassion Fatigue: A Review of Theoretical Terms, Risk Factors, and Preventive Methods for Clinicians and Researchers', *Best Practices in Mental Health: An International Journal,* 6(2): 57–68.

continuously 'using empathy' in their caring role, but in their case the recipient of this empathy is not a stranger but very often a close relative. The recipient is also 'suffering', whether from a specific disease or the general ills of advanced age. Thus, the daily experience of carers is a textbook illustration of the aspects of compassion fatigue. Somewhat surprisingly, this is not a topic often discussed in the context of Irish carers, although there is growing recognition of the problem in relation to health professionals, and various forms of training in techniques to promote resilience are available to them.

Although carers care for many reasons, the human values of compassion and empathy are at the forefront for a majority. 'Compassion' is defined in the *Merriam-Webster* dictionary as: 'sympathetic consciousness of others' distress together with a desire to alleviate it'. Carers witness the suffering and distress of their older relatives and instinctively want to alleviate it. It is this natural human instinct that carries many carers forward from day to day, week to week and year to year. If, however, due to compassion fatigue, the impetus gained from this instinct is depleted, caring becomes a much more difficult task. Research also identifies that compassion fatigue can be worsened for health professionals by the feeling that a client is not responding to treatment. For the carer of an older person who is at the end-of-life stage, there is no possibility of their relative recovering, and thus the potential for compassion fatigue is increased.

Experiencing compassion fatigue, of course, does not mean that carers *don't care*. The whole point is that they *do care*. What they are experiencing is a draining of their – limited – resources due to a situation that is too difficult or that has gone on for too long. While carers who experience compassion fatigue will very often continue to care for their relative, they may experience a feeling that 'their heart isn't in it any more'. Recognising that this is simply because they are, to put it in colloquial terms, 'running on empty', is a good first step toward taking action, and realising that this is a normal part of caring over a long period of time should give carers relief from the added sense of guilt they feel when they notice that they somehow care less than they used to.

Family carers and particularly those who have been caring for a long time should be aware of the symptoms of compassion fatigue. They can include:

- Emotional numbness and apathy
- Social withdrawal
- Exhaustion
- Resentment
- Self-medication
- Pessimism

The costs of compassion fatigue in family carers are high – for carers themselves, for the people they care for, and for society as a whole. One 2011 study in the US[56] on compassion fatigue in family caregivers of people with dementia found that:

> Informal caregivers for family members with dementia who develop compassion fatigue may terminate the caregiving relationship through premature nursing home admission ... and there may also be increased risk for abuse or neglect. Supporting these caregivers may improve outcomes for people with dementia ... and caring for family members at home provides a significant decrease in cost to society.

The same study found that family caregivers may be *more likely* than professionals to develop compassion fatigue, as a result of the particular combination of circumstances and responsibilities that prevent them from social engagement and self-care:

> the time caregivers spend on caregiving removes them from other relationships. Informal caregivers for family members with dementia often find themselves alone during the day with their family member, and, while this relationship is valuable, it does not replace peer relationships. Caregivers become isolated and often feel there is no one they can talk to about their feelings and that friends cannot relate to them. [A] survey of 30 caregivers found that caregivers felt resentful, helpless, and hopeless and that they had little free time. When a caregiver has little free time, they are unable to participate in activities focusing on themselves and fostering other relationships.

---

[56]　Day and Anderson (2011) 'Compassion Fatigue'.

As discussed above, resilience training is available for health professionals experiencing compassion fatigue, and similar training focused specifically on the caring role would be a valuable resource for long-term carers. Aspects of such training should include:

- Awareness of the concept of compassion fatigue
- Recognition of the signs of compassion fatigue
- Awareness of when and where to seek external help (for example, extra home care hours or extra community respite)
- Self-care techniques to tackle symptoms (for example, exercise or mindfulness)
- Techniques that promote resilience

The UK-based Crisis Prevention Institute is an international training organisation that supports the work of social services professionals and health professionals. They have listed 'Ten Laws Governing Healthy Caregiving',[57] some of which, although specifically directed at professionals rather than at family carers, can be applied to the family carer situation:

- Practice self-care daily
- Build a support system
- Recognise the humour
- Acknowledge your successes
- Remain optimistic
- Elevate levels of compassion satisfaction (compassion satisfaction is defined by Charles Figley as 'the ... joys derived from experiencing the suffering of others and succeeding in helping to relieve their suffering in some way')

Read more

- Compassion fatigue website: www.compassionfatigue.org
- Self-care for carers: www.selfcareforcarers.ie

---

[57]   http://www.compassionfatigue.org/pages/TheTenLawsHealthyCaregiving.pdf

CARER BURNOUT

'Burnout' is often described as existing on a continuum with compassion fatigue.[58] The term 'burnout' is generally applied to the negative psychological result of the perception that demands outweigh resources, or, as the *Oxford English Dictionary* defines it: 'physical or mental collapse caused by overwork or stress'. Compassion fatigue – the *emotional trauma* that results from the effort to help others – can contribute to burnout in carers. Carer burnout is one of the main reasons for the end of caring at home. It can be described as a state of exhaustion – mental, physical and emotional. It can be accompanied by feelings of fatigue, anxiety and depression, and can cause the carer to experience a feeling of resentment or unconcern toward the older person. The symptoms of carer burnout overlap with the symptoms of depression as well as with the symptoms of compassion fatigue, and, indeed, as mentioned, either or both of these may be contributing to the burnout. The symptoms of burnout include:

- Irritability and impatience
- Tearfulness and lack of pleasure in life
- Resentment toward the older person
- Lethargy
- Insomnia
- Exhaustion
- A feeling of being overwhelmed
- Drinking or smoking more than usual
- Social isolation
- Physical illnesses such as colds, flu and stomach bugs

Getting repeated minor illnesses may indicate a depleted immune system, while insomnia, irritability and tearfulness are indicators of depression. Insomnia leads to physical exhaustion. These may all feed into social withdrawal, where the carer feels no interest in meeting other people, especially

---

[58]   Sabo, B. (2011) 'Reflecting on the Concept of Compassion Fatigue', *The Online Journal of Issues in Nursing, 16(1)*, available from: http://ojin.nursingworld.org/Main MenuCategories/ANAMarketplace/ANAPeriodicals/OJIN/TableofContents/Vol-16-2011/No1-Jan-2011/Concept-of-Compassion-Fatigue.html.

people who don't understand what they're going through. Carers may also feel too tired to keep up hobbies and social activities that they previously enjoyed. Even time to themselves may bring no pleasure or decrease in stress. At this point there are serious indications of burnout.

It is in everybody's interest to avoid carer burnout. It is in the carer's interest, because at some stage the caring situation will end, but they may by then have acquired a chronic illness caused by the caring role. It is in the older person's interest, because if their family carers can no longer cope, the quality of their care will be reduced, or the only option may be nursing home care. It is in the interests of the wider family, because the carer's children, spouse/partner, siblings and friends will all be adversely affected by the carer experiencing burnout. It is in the state's interest, because ultimately the cost of care at home is a fraction of the cost of care in a nursing home, and secondly because, as previously discussed, burnout among carers is very likely to translate to increased healthcare costs 'downstream'.

Carer organisations offer advice on dealing with symptoms of burnout, with the most common advice being:

- Learn to recognise warning signs
- Ask for, and accept, help
- Learn about and link into available supports
- Eat well, rest where possible and exercise regularly
- Attend regular health checks
- Stay connected socially
- Establish a routine

This type of advice is common sense to a large extent, and in itself is excellent advice. However, responsibility for managing the issue is placed *on the carer themselves*. The problem with burnout is that neither time nor energy is available to the carer to follow the advice to exercise, attend social events, etc. It is vital that future developments in home care within the public health system do more to address the growing problem of carer burnout. And in order to recognise the potential for burnout, assessments of how carers are coping are *essential*. This is an issue where Ireland has so far failed woefully. Other countries, however, have excellent systems for evaluating how carers are coping, and we discuss these in the next section.

WHAT IRELAND CAN LEARN FROM OTHER COUNTRIES

Other countries have systems in place to measure the effects of caring on family carers with a view to avoiding burnout and compassion fatigue. Up to now, the needs of family carers have not been assessed in Ireland in any formal standardised way. An assessment tool called the Family Carer Needs Assessment has been developed, but progress in implementation is slow.[59] Questions included in such tools are designed to gather detailed information, including:

- The background to the caring situation and the needs of the older person
- Whether the carer lives with, or has to travel to, their relative, and how long the journey takes
- The support and help given by the carer
- The carer's own health, including mental health
- How caring affects the carer, including whether they feel able to cope
- The support the carer is receiving
- The carer's other commitments, including employment and family commitments (care of children/teenagers/another adult)
- The financial effect on the carer
- Plans for the future and contingency planning[60]

Other relevant questions include:

- Does the carer cope well emotionally with the caring role?
- How long has the caring situation been going on?

There are a range of tools currently in use in other countries to assess carer wellbeing, including the Carer Strain Index and the Zarit Burden Interview.

---

59   Care Alliance Ireland, *Public Provision of Home Care in Ireland – Update, October 2018*, available from: http://www.carealliance.ie/userfiles/file/Briefing%20Paper%20 2%20Web.pdf.

60   UK Government, Northern Ireland Single Assessment Tool: https://www.health-ni. gov.uk/publications/northern-ireland-single-assessment-tool-and-guidance.

The American Psychological Association has a range of online assessment tools. The Carer Support Needs Assessment Tool is a tool developed jointly by the University of Cambridge and the University of Manchester. It is used by carer services in the UK, Australia, Canada, the US and many other countries.

The US-based Family Caregiver Alliance advocates seven categories of information to be gathered in caregiver assessments:

- Background on the caregiver and the caregiving situation
- Caregiver's perception of health and functional status of the care recipient
- Caregiver's values and preferences with respect to everyday living and care provision
- Health and wellbeing of the caregiver
- Consequences of caregiving on the caregiver
- Care-provision requirements (skills, abilities, knowledge)
- Resources to support the caregiver

The background on the caregiver and the caregiving situation is important as it is designed to capture the history of caring within the family. As discussed previously, the public health system, often in the form of the public health nurse or social worker, may become involved in a family caring situation relatively late in the day. Family carers often manage low or moderate levels of care for many years without involving the public health system. The various health professionals may therefore be unaware of any history of caring within a family. The upshot is that by the time the public health system gets involved, perhaps at or near the end-of-life stage, the family carers may have been caring for years and may already be experiencing negative effects on their wellbeing.

In the UK, local authorities have a legal duty to assess the needs of any carer who requests this.[61] Under the 2014 Act, carers can apply to the local authority for an assessment of their needs. The UK National Health Service (NHS) website explains how this works:

---

[61]   NHS UK, Carers assessment: https://www.nhs.uk/conditions/social-care-and-support/carers-assessment/.

This assessment will consider the impact of caring on the carer. It will also consider the things a carer wants to achieve in their own day-to-day life. It must also consider other important issues, such as whether the carer is able or willing to carry on caring, whether they work or want to work, and whether they want to study or do more socially.

The assessments are carried out by trained staff from the local authority, and involve a one-to-one discussion between the carer and that staff member. The website suggests that before the assessment the carer might like to think about:

- Whether you want to continue being a carer
- If you are prepared to continue, what changes would make your life easier
- If there is any risk that you will not be able to continue as a carer without support
- Whether you have any physical or mental health problems, including stress or depression, which make your role as a carer more difficult
- Whether being a carer affects your relationships with other people, including family and friends
- If you are in paid work, whether being a carer causes problems at your work (such as often being late)
- If you like more time to yourself so that you can have a rest or enjoy some leisure activity
- If you like to do some training, voluntary work or paid work[62]

It is specified that the carer assessment should specifically look at:

- Parenting and childcare
- Marriage or other such relationships
- Friendships and community role
- Paid employment or voluntary work
- Interests, sport, leisure and hobbies

---

[62] NHS UK, Carers assessment: https://www.nhs.uk/conditions/social-care-and-support/carers-assessment/.

- Time for yourself[63]

In Scotland, carers also have the right to ask for an assessment, and support available can include, at the carer's choice: short breaks with or without the person cared for, help with housework, time to enjoy a hobby or see friends, emotional support, training to help in the caring role. Carers can also ask for re-assessments if their own circumstances or those of the person they care for change.

Read more

- Care Alliance Ireland, *Public Provision of Home Care in Ireland – Update*: https://www.carealliance.ie/Research
- Northern Ireland Carer Needs Assessment: https://www.health-ni.gov.uk/publications/northern-ireland-single-assessment-tool-and-guidance
- Scotland: Assessments: https://www.carersuk.org/images/Factsheets/Factsheet_S1020__Assessments_-_guide_to_getting_help.pdf

---

EMPLOYMENT INITIATIVES FOR FAMILY CARERS

The UK organisation Employers for Carers gives some startling figures for the impact of caring on employment:

1 in 9 people in every workplace is a carer and this figure is set to increase. Given the stresses and strains that can result from balancing work and caring, it is unsurprising that 1 in 6 carers give up work to care full-time. But many of these employees will be your most valuable staff, the 45–64-year-olds at the peak of their careers. By recognising the needs of carers, you can hold on to your experienced staff and reap the rewards of creating a supportive working environment for carers.

---

[63]   NHS UK, Carers assessment: https://www.nhs.uk/conditions/social-care-and-support/carers-assessment/.

This is echoed by the 2013 *Potential for Change* report[64] which says: 'With an estimated 2.3 million people having given up work to care, and a further 3 million having cut their hours, businesses are bearing the costs of a failure to support families to combine caring and work.'

The seriousness of the impact on the UK economy is forcing the state and employers to think about employment initiatives to facilitate family carers: 'Employers need to support working carers. Far from compromising business objectives, research shows that using a flexible working approach achieves impressive business results. Organisations that have introduced flexible working and special leave arrangements for carers have judged them a success. Their message is – it makes business sense to care for carers.'

The need for employment supports for carers is also a live issue in Ireland and was discussed in a 2018 research paper[65] looking at challenges in home care for older people. The paper refers to a European report showing that carers 'who can combine work and care report having a better quality of life and higher self-esteem than those who cannot'. In addition, these carers continue to be productive in the economy and to contribute to their own pensions and social protection entitlements. Some of the policy recommendations for carer–workers include:

- Income support and other 'flexicurity' measures
- Rights and regulations in the employment field
- Practical measures that can be implemented by employers at company level

With the chance now to implement a fit-for-purpose system of home care and supports for carers, a range of measures to enable family carers to continue in employment or self-employment should be considered as part of that new system.

---

[64] Carers UK, *Potential for Change*.
[65] Timoney, A. (2018) 'Home Care for Older People – Seven Policy Challenges', Dublin: Houses of the Oireachtas, available from: https://www.oireachtas.ie/parliament/media/housesoftheoireachtas/libraryresearch/spotlights/Spotlight_home_care_for_older_people_seven_policy_challenges_Jan_2018_101739.pdf.

Read more

- Anne Timoney, 'Home Care for Older People – Seven Policy Challenges': https://www.oireachtas.ie/parliament/media/housesofthe oireachtas/libraryresearch/spotlights/Spotlight_home_care_for_ older_people_seven_policy_challenges_Jan_2018_101739.pdf
- Employers for carers: https://www.employersforcarers.org/

17

The alternatives to family care at home

There may come a time when the older person is so frail that the family and perhaps the older person themselves begin to feel that nursing care rather than the general care provided by family or care workers is needed. Or it can happen that, given the circumstances, the family carers no longer have the capacity or finances to provide extensive care at home. Whatever the reasons, at this stage the question of alternatives must be considered.

Unfortunately, given the absence of a fit-for-purpose state home care scheme in Ireland at the moment, admission to residential care sometimes occurs for people who could be cared for at home. As discussed, the Department of Health is currently working on the creation of a new statutory home care scheme and it is to be hoped that this new scheme will go some way toward eliminating unnecessary admissions to residential care by greatly supplementing home care support. Organisations working for family carers in Ireland have been calling for such a scheme for many years. It remains to be seen what the outcome will be, but it looks likely that there will be a sea change in home care within the next number of years, hopefully making it possible for many more people to receive extensive care at home. This aspiration has been greatly strengthened by the 2020 Covid-19 pandemic.

PRIVATELY PURCHASED CARE AT HOME

If finances are available, then 24-hour nursing care can be privately purchased. Under the current system, the costs are prohibitive and beyond the reach of many families. Different companies have different charges, but 24-hour care, particularly night care and nursing care, runs into several thousand euro per month, generally quite a bit more than the full cost of nursing home care. The tax relief scheme discussed in Chapter 11 is available for the costs of home care, although Revenue figures suggest that the numbers availing of the scheme are low. The older person may have savings that can be used to pay some of the costs of home care, but a complication arises when the person's spouse/partner is still living, with the question then arising as to what their needs might be over the coming years, particularly if their outgoings exceed the fixed income they are receiving. This is another of the uncertainties discussed previously, and since there is no way of calculating what resources will be needed in the future, the safest course may be to safeguard a significant proportion of the available resources.

If the older person owns their own home, there is the possibility of equity release, that is, the taking out of a mortgage on part of the value of the house, to be paid off on the death of the mortgagor. However, if the older person's spouse/partner is living in the house, again this is more difficult and serious consideration must be given to safeguarding funds for the spouse/partner's possible future needs. Although equity release is possible in Ireland, careful consideration and professional financial advice would be required before entering such a scheme.

Another aspect to purchasing 24-hour home care is that there is likely to be a significant amount of coordination involved. Family carers must coordinate the care with the agency management and the home care workers themselves, ensure that relationships between the older person and the care workers are good, sort out any problems that arise, liaise with health professionals, etc.

RESIDENTIAL CARE

Factors in the decision on residential care

The other main alternative is for the older person to move to residential care. The 2020 Covid pandemic has heightened this issue for many families, and some have removed older relatives from nursing home care. The tragedy of the numerous deaths of older people in nursing homes during the pandemic has made families and older people frightened of the option of residential care and brought the state's relationship with the private nursing home sector under the spotlight. What is clear is that the state must take greater responsibility for older people in private care homes, including clarifying lines of responsibility for the health of residents.

Even before the pandemic, the decision around nursing home care for older people was understandably an emotive one for many. The older person may not wish to leave their home. Families may feel they have failed their older relative if they have to consider it. For many families, it is a last resort, considered when all other reasonable alternatives have been exhausted. Families who have cared for their older relatives at home to the best of their ability should not see the move to a nursing home as a failure. We discussed in the Introduction how research has shown that the preference of the great majority of older people is to remain at home 'for as long as possible', and how this is also the preference of many families, and of the state. The decision that the older person should be cared for in a nursing home is often taken, in the current circumstances in Ireland, because the limits of what is possible have been reached. The heavy time, energy and financial requirements of intensive long-term home care, with the current low level of support available from the state, is pushing family carers toward the decision. This is borne out by research:[66] 'The home help service has no

---

[66]   Wren, M.A., Normand, C., O'Reilly, D., Cruise, S., Connolly, S. and Murphy, C. (2012) *Towards the Development of a Predictive Model of Long-term Care Demand*

statutory basis and its patchy provision, combined with the system of state subsidy for residential care, biases utilisation towards residential care.'

For many families, the decision is an extremely difficult one, especially if they have been able to keep the older person at home through a long period of significant dependency and intensive caring.

Gathering information

The decision around a move to nursing home care should be approached like other decisions, in that acquiring as much relevant information as possible and talking to people who can provide considered objective insights allow the question to be approached rationally. All aspects need consideration, and a knee-jerk reaction based purely on emotion should be avoided. When the issue begins to come up for discussion, the older person, if they are not too ill, should of course be consulted first. The older person's spouse/partner should be involved in the discussion at all times, if possible. Useful insights may also be available from:

- A geriatric consultant
- The older person's GP
- The public health nurse
- Friends who have relatives living in nursing homes

After consultation with medical professionals, it may be clear that the medical or care needs of the older person are such that nursing care from professional staff is in the older person's best interests.

It is useful also at this stage to draw up a list of suitable homes and visit them (see further information below). Knowing a little more about the actual places being considered may help with the decision, as you may get a favourable (or unfavourable) impression from a visit to the physical premises.

---

for *Northern Ireland and the Republic of Ireland,* Queen's University Belfast/Trinity College Dublin.

Balancing interests

If a nursing home is being considered partly because of the cost of the caring effort for the family, its effects on other dependents of the family carers – children, teenagers and any other dependent adults – should be explored at this stage. The effect on carers' spouses/partners should also be taken into account. Any effects on the health and wellbeing of the family carers should be included in this discussion, as well as any adverse consequences they may be experiencing in their working lives.

The financial aspect should also be considered, particularly if financial resources need to be conserved for the older person's spouse/partner. In relation to the cost of nursing home care, the Fair Deal scheme, although not universally popular, at least places a cap on the cost of care.

The best outcome is a decision in which the interests of everybody involved are considered, and a balanced decision reached. There is no right or wrong answer here; there is simply a decision reached after careful consideration.

HIQA inspection reports and complaints to HIQA

As stated, this book was written before the 2020 Covid-19 pandemic and it is both too soon and beyond the scope of the book to analyse the factors involved in the disastrous outcome of the pandemic for many nursing home residents. It is likely that the nursing home sector will undergo significant changes in the coming years in light of the tragedy. However, for the time being, the system is still in place and so we discuss the current situation in the following sections.

Some of the emotion around the move to a nursing home stems from the scandals about neglect, failures in care and even abuse in nursing homes and other residential institutions. Many people will remember the Leas Cross scandal of 2005, which led to the setting up of the Health Information and Quality Authority (HIQA), and the more recent Áras Attracta scandal. Since the setting up of HIQA, nursing homes have become more regulated, and, on recent figures,[67] 90 per cent were inspected by HIQA staff in 2017. However, this means that 10 per cent of homes were not inspected, and, of

---

[67]   https://www.rte.ie/news/ireland/2018/0729/981446-hiqa-complaints/

course, an inspection observes conditions in homes on one day. This level of inspection is clearly not adequate, given that in 2017, 680 complaints were made to HIQA about failures of care in nursing homes.[68] HIQA agrees that legislation is needed to safeguard vulnerable adults in residential care, and the Adult Safeguarding Bill 2017 is currently before the Seanad.

HIQA reports are published online for every nursing home in the country, and can be consulted by the public. HIQA inspectors base their findings on the relevant regulations under the legislation, and on the *National Standards for Residential Care Settings for Older People in Ireland*.

Each inspection and report focuses on specific 'outcomes', for example:

- Outcome 02: Governance and Management
- Outcome 04: Suitable Person in Charge
- Outcome 07: Safeguarding and Safety
- Outcome 09: Medication Management
- Outcome 18: Suitable Staffing

Homes inspected are judged to be 'Compliant', 'Substantially Compliant', 'Non-Compliant – Moderate', etc. Where risks are found or recommendations are made following findings of non-compliance, these are followed up by inspectors at subsequent inspections. In cases of serious non-compliance, HIQA has the power to close down homes.

In the light of this regime, it is more difficult to hide substandard care now than it was in the past. All nursing homes are judged against national standards, and levels of care must reach these standards in all respects. The fact that the information is easily accessed online by the public means that it is imperative for homes to reach these standards, even viewed purely from a business point of view. Reports have found that public confidence in nursing homes has significantly increased since the establishment of HIQA. That is not to say that neglect and abuse no longer occur in nursing homes, and some of the complaints made to HIQA in 2017 are extremely disturbing. The Department of Health stated in December 2017 that a new National Adult Safeguarding Policy would be developed for the health sector.

---

68   https://www.rte.ie/news/ireland/2018/0729/981446-hiqa-complaints/

A final word regarding family worries about substandard care: the visible presence of family members visiting at unexpected times is the best safeguard against neglect and a good way to prompt excellent care. We are all aware, perhaps subconsciously, when our work is being observed and evaluated, and we automatically adjust to expectations. Family members showing interest and engaging with staff over the care of their relative will prompt the best care for the older person. Positive engagement should have a better outcome: if something is a problem for care staff, you may be able to help resolve it, making life easier for both your relative and their carers. This sort of teamwork should prompt the best care for your relative, rather than taking an approach that looks for problems to criticise. For occasions when problems do arise, homes should have a clear complaints procedure, and asking to see this should form part of your inspection of possible nursing homes (see more on this in the next sections).

Some benefits of residential care

This section would not be complete without consideration of the benefits that many people experience in good quality residential care. In Ireland, we have not yet come to accept and implement the concept of retirement villages and other types of sheltered housing (although there was some discussion of this at government level in 2018), and so residential care in the main consists of nursing home care. The benefits that care in good quality nursing homes can provide must be considered.

The social aspect of residential care may be especially beneficial to older people who have been living alone or have been housebound. Many homes provide outings, exercise classes, art classes, music, and other forms of entertainment, and many will also facilitate religious services. Most nursing homes provide quality nursing care, and the publicly available HIQA reports provide detailed information on this aspect of homes. Meals served to residents are (or should be) carefully planned for their nutritional value and attractiveness. Staff in nursing homes are required to be trained and vetted.

For some people nursing homes may provide more physical comfort than is possible at home, as the homes will have equipment to facilitate showering, hair washing and other forms of personal care that may be difficult at home. Nursing homes provide hairdressing and chiropody services on a regular basis. In addition, they often provide physiotherapy, occupational therapy and speech therapy on the premises. Where older people have severe mobility difficulties and require assistance from one or perhaps two people when walking, there will be trained staff available to make sure that the older person gets as many assisted walks as recommended. Again, it may be difficult in the home situation to ensure that the older person gets enough exercise to retain the mobility that they have if two people are required to assist them.

Some homes have gardens where residents can sit out. Residents can bring their own belongings to create a familiar, comfortable environment. The *National Guidelines for Residential Care Settings for Older People* contains provisions regarding the 'homeliness' of nursing homes; it defines 'homely' as: 'simple but cosy and comfortable, as in one's own home', and further states: 'The physical environment in the residential care service should be as comfortable and homely as possible. Furnishings and facilities [should be] homely. Residents [should be] facilitated to decorate their area of personal space with furnishings from home.'

There is further discussion below of the move away from nursing homes as institutions and toward the 'household model' and person-centred care. In summary, it is important to consider objectively the benefits that care in a good nursing home could provide to a very frail older person.

Of course, a move to a nursing home does not mean that family carers are no longer carers. Carers in this phase are known as 'transitional carers'. Many family carers visit their relatives daily, helping with some of the tasks they did at home such as helping with meals, looking after clothes, taking their relative out or for walks within the home. And since they no longer have all the caring responsibilities they used to have, family carers are freer to provide companionship by watching TV with their relative, reading to them, sharing a crossword, or whatever they used to do at home.

Read more

- Health Information Quality Authority: Inspection Reports for Irish nursing homes: https://www.hiqa.ie/reports-and-publications/inspection-reports?field_centre_type_target_id=41&tid_1=All&keys=&field_county_value=All

- HIQA: *National Standards for Residential Care Settings for Older People in Ireland*: https://www.hiqa.ie/sites/default/files/2017-01/National-Standards-for-Older-People.pdf
- HIQA: report a concern to HIQA: https://www.hiqa.ie/get-touch/report-concern

---

Finding a suitable nursing home

Many things need to be considered when it comes to choosing a nursing home, one of the main factors being location. Should the nursing home be near the older person's home, where perhaps their friends can easily visit, or should it be near to where adult children live? Is the older person's spouse/partner able to visit independently? Are there good transport links to the home for any family members who don't drive? Once a decision has been made on the best location, a list of homes in the area/s chosen can be found on the HSE/HIQA websites. Ask anyone you think might be familiar with the homes for their impressions. When you have identified a few possibilities, read the HIQA reports[69] on each, looking in detail at the very positive and very negative aspects. In particular, where a recommendation has been made in one HIQA review, check to see that it has been dealt with in the next report. Where HIQA recommendations are not followed up, there may be problems with the management of the home, and this would need further investigation. Ring to request a brochure for the homes you select.

Next, make an appointment to visit the homes, and again, a visit by two or more people is best: the older person, if possible, their spouse/partner, and one or more family carers. You will be shown around the home by a member of staff, and you can ask questions and ask to see the care home policies. It is useful to have decided in advance exactly what questions you want to ask and to have a list of them with you. Look at arrangements for meals and for entertainment. You may also like to make a second visit on a different day at a different time. If you have concerns as a result of reading the inspection reports, raise these at the meeting. The HSE has published the very useful *Guide to Choosing a Private Nursing Home*, which you can

---

[69] https://www.hiqa.ie/reports-and-publications/inspection-reports?field_centre_type_target_id=41&tid_1=All&keys=&field_county_value=All

read at: http://www.hse.ie/eng/services/list/4/olderpeople/residentialcare/ Nursinghomechecklist.pdf.

Checklist 17.1 presents a list of essential elements to look out for when visiting nursing homes, and a list of suggested questions is given in Checklist 17.2.

Checklist 17.1: Initial impressions of home/things to look out for

- Is the home clean and tidy?
- Do the residents look well cared for?
- Is there a pleasant atmosphere?
- Is the overall décor fresh?
- Do the residents seem active or are many just sitting around?
- Are the staff you pass by friendly?
- Are there any trip risks and do you feel that health and safety factors are well attended to?
- Do you feel welcome?
- Does the reception display good information for relatives and visitors such as meal times, etc.?
- Do you get the impression that visitors are welcomed?
- Are there any unpleasant smells?
- Are there lists of activities displayed?
- Do you feel that the residents' privacy is respected?

The following is a list of questions you might like to ask during a visit, and you can add to this depending on the particular circumstances that apply to you and your relative. The HSE guide mentioned above contains numerous other questions that you may need to ask.

Checklist 17.2: Sample questions to ask when viewing a nursing home

- Are there single/shared rooms available?
- How many residents are there?
- How many day staff are there, and how many night staff?
- Are there extra charges for medical equipment such as a medical bed?
- What medical attention is available?

- What entertainments are available? Is there an extra charge?
- Is there a garden for the residents?
- What personal care is available – chiropody, hairdressing, etc.?
- Is physiotherapy/speech therapy/occupational therapy available?

Read more

- HSE: Nursing Home checklist: https://www.hse.ie/eng/services/list/4/olderpeople/residentialcare/nursinghomechecklist.pdf

---

The move to nursing home care

Carers can do several things to make the move to a nursing home run smoothly and to make it as easy as possible for the older person. Preparing both yourself and your relative over a period of time may help, such as looking at brochures, showing them photos of the interior, or discussing the routine and events within the home. Visits to the home before the move may help some older people, allowing them to get to know staff and some of the residents. Some people may prefer not to talk about the move at all, adopting a sort of avoidance approach, and this should be accepted. Remember that the move essentially involves your relative moving to a strange place to live among strangers, and be as understanding as possible.

The HSE *Guide to Choosing a Private Nursing Home* offers practical advice on the actual move, and recommends having the following information available when arranging for admission:

- Information on medical history
- Information on current health status
- A list of current medicines
- A list of all your healthcare providers
- A list of family members to call in case of emergency
- Payment information for nursing home office staff

Other preparations can include:

- Creating a homely atmosphere by placing familiar items such as rugs, cushions etc. in the bedroom at the home, hanging photographs of family members on the walls, and arranging ornaments on shelves.
- Bringing a favourite chair or other small piece of furniture for the room.
- Some homes like to receive a life history book about their new resident so that staff have opportunities for conversation and can get to know them more quickly. This could include details of their upbringing, family, interests, working life, pets, travel, etc.

Read more

- Alzheimer Scotland: *Letting Go Without Giving Up: Continuing to Care for the Person with Dementia*: https://www.alzscot.org/sites/default/files/images/0000/0275/lettinggo.pdf
- Care UK: moving to a nursing home: https://www.careuk.com/sites/rcs/files/Care_UK_rcs__Moving_checklist.pdf

The household model and person-centred care

Countries worldwide are grappling with the issue of long-term care, and new ideas are being put forward with a view to moving away from nursing homes as 'institutions' and toward the creation of homes with more emphasis on the 'home' part of the term 'nursing home'. One study from the Netherlands[70] describes the evolution of the idea neatly:

> Nursing home care used to be primarily organized according to a medical care concept in traditional large-scale wards with an institutional character. Physical care needs were the main focus of attention and care for people with dementia was organized around routines of the nursing staff.

---

[70]   de Boer, B., Hamers, J.P.H., Beerens, H.C., Zwakhalen, S.M.G., Tan F.E.S. and Verbeek, H. (2015) 'Living at the Farm, Innovative Nursing Home Care for People with Dementia – Study Protocol of an Observational Longitudinal Study', *BMC Geriatrics*, 15, (144).

The authors note the current move toward 'person-centred' care:

> In many countries, current nursing homes are increasingly organized according to a psychosocial and more homelike care concept. Here, the care is often organized in smaller units, usually with 6–8 residents. The residents live together in a homelike and recognizable environment in which striving to achieve a situation closest to home is the priority. Personal care and daily routines are integrated, meaning that care staff perform tasks such as cooking and cleaning together with the residents. This psychosocial care concept strives to allow people to continue the life they had before admission, as much as possible, and promotes person-centred care and quality of life. In addition, this type of care involves the provision of autonomy for residents, letting them make their own choices and encouraging social interaction and participation in activities.

The US is in the vanguard of this 'de-institutionalisation' process. The concepts of person-centred care and the 'household model' are being explored. As an example, everyone in an 'institution' has meals at the same time, while the household model allows residents to choose when to sleep, eat, etc. Other elements of the household model include the elimination of the nursing station, on the basis that it creates a separation between residents and staff. Smaller desks in alcoves or living areas provide the necessary organisation without the institutional 'look'.

Other ideas focus on keeping homes small, with private bedrooms and bathrooms arranged around communal kitchen and living areas. Assistants help the residents to prepare food and do light housework. The concept of 'elder-friendly communities' with nursing care is emerging in the US. Ideas being trialled include the presence of cats, dogs and birds in the home, as well as co-siting nursing homes and preschools. Currently there are 'intergenerational centres' with co-sited facilities for older people and preschool children in Japan, Canada and the USA.

A more unusual concept in the care of older people (although it is already being used for people with mental health issues and addictions) is the green care farm. The Dutch study mentioned above found that in the Netherlands there are approximately 200 green care farms providing day care for people with dementia, and a recent expansion of this is the establishment of small nursing home units on green care farms.

Another small innovation in the move away from care homes as institutions is improved activities for residents – a move 'beyond bingo' – including: wine and cheese nights, cooking, knitting or baking for local community organisations, gardening clubs, personalised music playlists, YouTube hour, virtual travel.

In Ireland the discussion on alternatives to the traditional nursing home is at an early stage, but will no doubt be expedited by the 2020 Covid pandemic. Some discussion has already taken place. In 2018 the Department of Health and the Department of Housing, Planning and Local Government held discussions about working together regarding the provision of state-funded villages for older people, and in November 2018 the Minister for Older People announced a 20-year plan to replace nursing homes with retirement villages with various levels of assistance available for residents. Although such policies are not universally accepted, they offer another choice for older people and their carers, and they may well suit many older people.

Read more

- The Green House Project: https://www.thegreenhouseproject.org/about/discover
- '"Would You Do That in Your Home?" Making Nursing Homes Home-like in Culture Change Implementation' https://www.ncbi.nlm.nih.gov/pmc/articles/PMC5363857/

18

When caring ends

Grief, relief, guilt

Most often, caring at home comes to an end when the older person passes away, and family carers will experience the grief of the loss of a close relative. When the older person has suffered significantly during their final years or months, a strong feeling of relief may accompany the grief – relief that the older person's suffering has come to an end, and relief that perhaps a very difficult period in their own lives has come to an end. This emotion is surprising both to carers themselves and to others, and carers may feel guilty for feeling relieved and try to hide it. However, studies in the field of caring have shown that relief is an entirely normal and extremely common emotion for family carers. Just knowing that what they are feeling is both 'normal' and common may help some carers to deal with their feelings of guilt. There may also, for some carers, be a sense that they are not as bereft as they had anticipated, and again, this can prompt feelings of guilt. But an explanation can be found in the particular circumstances of the older person's death: they may have had poor or very poor quality of life, they may have welcomed their own approaching death or suffered significantly for an extended period of time. Perhaps death was anticipated for a long time. As discussed above in the section on anticipatory grief, family members begin to grieve when terminal decline begins, so that when death occurs they may have already gone through a long period of grieving. In addition, family may have lost sight of the person they knew, as the older person became increasingly dependent and ceased to interact normally with them. As the end-of-life period proceeds, the older person may withdraw into themselves, speaking little and showing limited awareness of those around them. For this period, the much loved mother, father, aunt, uncle or grandparent may 'disappear', to be replaced by a frail person whose needs are the focus of the family's attention. People have described this as a 'fading away', and indeed, the older person's personality does fade as they become more frail and weak. Thus, although the family 'loses' their relative on death, in reality they may have lost him or her a long time previously.

The other way that full-time caring ends is if the older person moves to residential care. However, in this situation, family members may still carry out many caring activities, such as visiting regularly, advocating for their relative in the home, liaising with staff and medical personnel, participating in care plan meetings, keeping the older person company, taking them on outings if possible, etc. Family members in this situation may still spend many hours per week with their relative – they are still carers. People in this situation are sometimes called 'transitional carers'.

LIFE AFTER CARING

It can be very difficult to pick up the pieces after caring, particularly when the carer has cared full-time for a close relative for a considerable length of time. Some family carers, especially full-time carers, experience the sense of a gaping hole in their lives when their caring role ends. The death of the older person of course means a complete end to the caring role, and so carers must cope with grief and bereavement, and deal with practical matters in relation to the death, as well as trying to envisage a life for themselves in the future.

Available support

Fortunately, this problem is well recognised by carer organisations, and resources and advice are available. Much of the advice comes directly from former carers with personal experience of this sense of loss and uncertainty. Care Alliance Ireland published a comprehensive booklet for former carers in 2018, which can be downloaded at the link below or obtained by phoning their offices. Called *The Way Ahead*,[71] the booklet is aimed mainly at full-time carers whose older relative has died. The booklet contains practical information on:

- Registering a death
- Bereavement counselling
- Coping with finances and wills
- Returning to work or retraining
- Filling the void left by the end of the caring role

Staff in local carers organisations will also be able to help and answer questions, and again, many such staff either are or have been carers themselves and have an excellent understanding of such challenges.

Skills acquired during caring that transfer to the workplace

Family carers rarely recognise the multiple skills they acquire through their caring role, but these have been collated by carers organisations. Table 18.1 and Figure 18.1 show the range of skills carers can acquire through their role – skills that are transferable to the workplace.

Volunteering and mentoring

Many former carers find volunteering for a time with carers organisations valuable, allowing them to pass their expertise on to new carers, and to feel a sense of achievement in the skills they have acquired while caring. Family Carers Ireland runs a mentorship programme for new carers and a

---

71   Care Alliance Ireland (2018) The Way Ahead, available from: https://www.care alliance.ie/userfiles/file/The%20Way%20Ahead%20Web%20SP.pdf.

befriending programme for older adults. Contact your local Family Carers Ireland office to volunteer.

Figure 18.1: Skills that carers have to offer employers

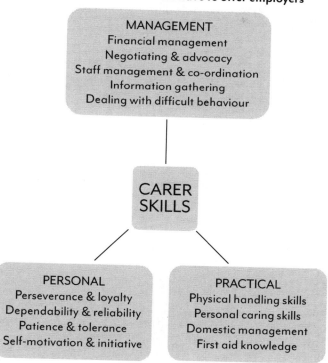

MANAGEMENT
Financial management
Negotiating & advocacy
Staff management & co-ordination
Information gathering
Dealing with difficult behaviour

CARER SKILLS

PERSONAL
Perseverance & loyalty
Dependability & reliability
Patience & tolerance
Self-motivation & initiative

PRACTICAL
Physical handling skills
Personal caring skills
Domestic management
First aid knowledge

Source: adapted from Care Alliance Ireland

The expertise of former carers is invaluable to carers organisations. While health professionals and researchers in the field can do so much, it is those at the coalface, carers themselves, who can offer the best and most welcome advice to other carers.

Table 18.1: Skills acquired by family carers that are transferable to the workplace

Tasks	Working with Data	Working with People	Working with Things	Working with Ideas
Personal care		Sensitivity	Using specialist equipment	Time management
Organising respite care	Budgeting/ research skills	Liaison skills	Telephone skills	Assessment/ problem-solving skills
Arranging daily activities		Ability to work as part of a team		Organisational skills
Meetings/ reviews		Negotiation skills		Planning skills
Benefit applications	Detailed presentation of information	Assertiveness	Administration skills/form filling	Ability to present ideas in writing
Benefit check	Problem solving		Keeping accurate records	
Finding out about the disability or illness	Research skills	Communication skills		Transport
Knowledge of the local area			Driving a vehicle	
Managing behaviour		Communication skills	Ability to use safe restraint techniques	Adaptability/ flexibility
Visits to doctor/ hospital	Presentation/ understanding of information	Communication skills		Ability to ask relevant questions

Source: Care Alliance Ireland

Read more

- Care Alliance Ireland: *The Way Ahead*: https://www.carealliance.ie/userfiles/file/The%20Way%20Ahead%20Web%20SP.pdf
- Citizens Information: when someone dies: http://www.citizensinformation.ie/en/death/when_someone_dies_in_ireland.html
- Family Carers Ireland: volunteer with us: https://familycarers.ie/get-involved/volunteer-with-us/

Resources

Note: These resources are listed for information only and do not necessarily represent the author's views. Use appropriate security software when accessing the internet.

BLOGS

Many of the private home care agencies regularly publish useful blogs containing practical information for carers; see the websites of home care agencies for examples. Some carers, many US based, have created private blogs which are useful for discussions of issues that are not raised in more formal blogs.

- A Carer's Voice: http://www.acarersvoice.com/a-carers-voice/carers-blogs/
- CareGiving.com: https://www.caregiving.com
- Caring.com: https://www.caring.com/
- EldercareABCBlog: http://eldercareabcblog.com/
- The Caregiver Space: http://thecaregiverspace.org/

Live Better With Dementia is a site for older people with dementia and their carers: https://dementia.livebetterwith.com/

Carers organisations

Ireland

Care Alliance Ireland   www.carealliance.ie/

Family Carers Ireland   https://familycarers.ie/

The Palliative Hub   www.carers.thepalliativehub.com

UK

Carers UK   www.carersuk.org/

Europe

European Association Working for www.eurocarers.org/
Carers

International

Carers Australia   www.carersaustralia.com.au/

Family Caregiver Alliance (US)   www.caregiver.org/

International Alliance of Carer   www.internationalcarers.org/
Organisations

Young carers

Together for Young Adult Carers   www.youngadultcarers.eu/

Financial and legal advice

Organisation	Website	Telephone
Citizens Information	http://www.citizensinformation.ie/en/	0761 07 4000
Family Carers Ireland Legal Advice	https://familycarers.ie/help-and-advice/legal-advice/	1800 240 724
Free Legal Advice Centre	https://www.flac.ie/	1890 350 250
Money Advice and Budgeting Service	www.mabs.ie	0761 07 2000

GENERAL RESOURCES

Organisation	Website	Telephone
Citizens Information Service	http://www.citizensinformation.ie/en/	0761 07 4000
Disabled Drivers Association	https://www.ddai.ie/	094 936 4045/ 094 936 4266/ 01 810 3794
Irish Wheelchair Association	www.iwa.ie	01 818 6400

HEALTH RESOURCES

Resource	Website
Care givers resource from the Multiple Sclerosis society	https://www.ms-society.ie/pages/living-with-ms/carers-
Chime (formerly DeafHear)	www.chime.ie
HSE services for older people	https://www.hse.ie/eng/services/list/4/olderpeople/
How to protect yourself against falls, HSE	http://www.hse.ie/eng/services/list/4/olderpeople/tipsforhealthyliving/slipstripsfalls.html

ORGANISATIONS FOR OLDER PEOPLE

Organisation	Website	Telephone
Active Retirement Ireland	http://www.activeirl.ie/	01 873 3836
Age Action	https://www.ageaction.ie/	01 475 6989
ALONE	http://alone.ie/	01 679 1032

The Alzheimer Society of Ireland	http://www.alzheimer.ie/Home.aspx	01 207 3800
Friends of the Elderly Ireland	https://friendsoftheelderly.ie/	01 873 1855
Irish Senior Citizens' Parliament	https://iscp.wordpress.com/about/	–
Sage Advocacy	https://www.sageadvocacy.ie/	1850719400
Third Age	http://www.thirdageireland.ie/	046 955 7766

TRAINING RESOURCES

Organisation/Training Area	Website
Acquired Brain Injury Ireland	https://www.abiireland.ie/
The Alzheimer Society of Ireland	https://www.alzheimer.ie/
Dementia Elevator (dementia training)	http://dementiaelevator.ie/blog/2015/11/22/dementia-coping-skills-for-families-and-carers/
Family Carers Ireland	https://familycarers.ie/help-and-advice/training/
Family Carer Training (Care Alliance Ireland)	http://www.familycarertraining.ie/Online-courses
The Open University: Caring for Adults	http://www.open.edu/openlearncreate/course/view.php?id=2171
Understand Together dementia training	https://www.understandtogether.ie/training-resources/dementia-training-and-education/

Selected bibliography

Care Alliance Ireland (2018) *Briefing Paper 2: Public Provision of Home Care in Ireland – Update, October 2018*, available from: http://www.carealliance.ie/userfiles/file/Briefing%20Paper%202%20Web.pdf.

Central Statistics Office (2016) 'Census of Population 2016 – Profile 9 Health, Disability and Carers', available from: www.cso.ie/en/releasesandpublications/ep/p-cp9hdc/p8hdc/.

Family Carers Ireland (2018) *Carer's Companion: Information and Advice for Family Carers in Ireland from Family Carers Ireland*, available from: https://familycarers.ie/carer-supports/help-advice/carers-companion#:~:text=The%20Carer's%20Companion%20is%20a,most%20stressful%20and%20isolating%20time.

Figley, C. (1995) *Compassion Fatigue: Coping with Secondary Traumatic Stress Disorder in Those who Treat the Traumatized*, New York: Brunner/Routledge.

Freedman, David H., 'Health Care's "Upstream" Conundrum', *Politico*, 10 January 2018, available from: https://www.politico.com/agenda/story/2018/01/10/long-term-health-nation-problems-000613.

General Medical Council (2020) *Treatment and Care Towards the End of Life: Good Practice in Decision Making*, available from: https://www.gmc-uk.org/ethical-guidance/ethical-guidance-for-doctors/treatment-and-care-towards-the-end-of-life/cardiopulmonary-resuscitation-cpr.

Government of Ireland (2012) *National Carers' Strategy*, Dublin, available from: http://health.gov.ie/wp-content/uploads/2016/02/National-Carers-Strategy.pdf.

Groen, H. (2017) *The Secret Diary of Hendrik Groen, 83¼ Years Old*, The Netherlands: Penguin Books.

Groen, H. (2018) *On the Bright Side: The New Secret Diary of Hendrik Groen*, The Netherlands: Penguin Books.

Hanley, P. and Sheerin, C. (2017) 'Valuing Informal Care in Ireland: Beyond the Traditional Production Boundary', *Economic and Social Review* 48(3): 337–364.

HSE *Protecting Older People from Abuse*, Dublin, available from: https://www.hse.ie/eng/services/list/4/olderpeople/carersrelatives/protecting-older-people-from-abuse.html.

HSE (2010) *National Guidelines & Procedures for Standardised Implementation of the Home Care Packages Scheme*, available from: http://lenus.ie/hse/bitstream/10147/120850/1/hcpsguidelines.pdf.

HSE (2016) *Activity & Resource Review: Home Care Services May 2016*, available from: http://hdl.handle.net/10147/621444.

Lafferty, A. Fealy, G. Downes, C. and Drennan, J. (2014) *Family Carers of Older People: Results of a National Survey of Stress, Conflict and Coping*, Dublin: NCPOP, University College Dublin.

Law Reform Commission (2008) 'Bioethics: Advance Care Directives Consultation Paper', *LRC CP 51*.

Migrant Rights Centre of Ireland (2015) *Migrant Workers in the Home Care Sector: Preparing for the Elder Boom in Ireland*, available from: http://www.mrci.ie/.

O'Neill, D. (2013) *Ageing and Caring*, Dublin: Orpen Press.

Rosenthal, G. and Salamon, M.J. (1990) *Home or Nursing Home: Making the Right Choices*, New York: Springer Publishing.

Sabo, B. (2011) 'Reflecting on the Concept of Compassion Fatigue', *The Online Journal of Issues in Nursing* 16(1), available from: http://ojin.nursingworld.org/MainMenuCategories/ANAMarketplace/ANAPeriodicals/OJIN/TableofContents/Vol-16-2011/No1-Jan-2011/Concept-of-Compassion-Fatigue.html.

Thiel, L. (2016) *Caring Alone? Social Capital and the Mental Health of Caregivers*, Berlin: German Institute for Economic Research.

Timoney, A. (2018) 'Home Care for Older People – Seven Policy Challenges', *Spotlight* 1, available from: https://www.oireachtas.ie/parliament/media/housesoftheoireachtas/libraryresearch/spotlights/Spotlight_home_care_for_older_people_seven_policy_challenges_Jan_2018_101739.pdf.

Ziemba, R.A. (2002) 'Family Health & Caring for Elderly Parents', *Michigan Family Review* 7(1): 35–52.